Kitchen Living

Kitchen Interiors for Contemporary Homes

gestalten

Bringing More to the Table

Food writer Mina Holland muses on the changing role of cooking spaces

For a long time, I didn't have a kitchen. While my partner and I were saving for our flat, we lived at his mom's house. A kitchen of our own was a concept, a mental sketch roughly colored in by a dowry of possessions collected during years of anticipation. I had, among other things, a sharp knife wrapped in an old tea towel, a Charles and Diana commemorative mug bought at a charity shop (this republican's single concession to the British monarchy), and a stash of jam jars filled with various spices that gave off a dubious incense. These things lived in cardboard boxes but, more importantly, they occupied an imaginary space that was our one-day kitchen.

There is more significance to this than I knew at the time. So much of what the kitchen now represents is imaginative, intangible. While there was obviously a kitchen at my mother-in-law's—a room for food preparation—we

→ *British food writer Mina Holland is pictured at home in her kitchen in Crofton Park, south London, where she lives together with her husband Freddie and their dog Ernie.*

didn't have a space of our own to fulfill all the other functions that a kitchen might have: somewhere to gather, to host, to toast, to make introductions, to feed, to potter, to laugh, to discuss, to quarrel, to learn, and to express ourselves with the things we choose to own, to cook, and to talk about. I couldn't wait to push the colored spines of my cookbooks into a designated shelf, to click my knives onto a wall magnet, to pile my ceramic plates pleasingly in a cupboard. Even more than this, I couldn't wait for the conversations that would happen in there, to listen to the radio with breakfast, to have a friend sit drinking wine while I made a pasta sauce. These were my ordinary domestic fantasies, but fantasies they were.

In the past, kitchens were hidden away and served a simple, unglamorous purpose, while public life took place in reception rooms. Whatever your social class, entertaining would have happened away from the kitchen until well into the Victorian era, and is perhaps most starkly represented by the televised period dramas portraying "upstairs downstairs" culture: downstairs kitchens were the dark, clattering, fat-scented domains of servants who prepared the dishes their employers would enjoy upstairs, in drawing and dining rooms flooded with natural light and the best furniture. How times have changed! Practically and symbolically, the kitchen has transcended straightforward culinary utility: it is the nucleus of a home. And now that I have a home, with a kitchen, it's where most of waking life happens. Though we might wander to another room to wash or sleep, the kitchen always draws us back with its smells, its tastes, its noises, and by the promise of action.

To grasp the symbolic role of the kitchen, it's important to first understand the emotive power of food for human beings, beyond being fuel for the body. Cooking—and learning to cook—is only partially a question of skill and know-how; the American food writer Paula Wolfert once told me that she learned recipes in Morocco "with kisses, cuddles, and measuring

→ *As we spend more and more time in the kitchen, we increasingly decorate the space with the colors and textures that were once more characteristic of a living room.*

"Practically and symbolically, the kitchen has transcended straightforward culinary utility: it is *the nucleus of a home*"

spoons." The making, giving, and sharing of food are acts of love, and, I think, the most powerful source of non-verbal communication. For what other reason do we fondly remember our late grandmother's shepherd's pie? How else can food transport us to another time and place as much as madeleine cakes did for Proust's Marcel? Why otherwise would I crave something so apparently underwhelming as a baked potato, a family staple, when I feel in need of home comfort? As literary critic Sandra M. Gilbert writes in *The Culinary Imagination*, "The pulse of the kitchen is the pulse of human life, which triumphs over death by turning nature into nurture, and, often, the raw into the cooked." Or, as my husband paraphrases, "If home is where the heart is, the kitchen is the aorta."

The kitchen, then, has literally and metaphorically opened up in recent years. Perhaps partly in response to the proliferation of fast and convenience foods, not to mention improved consciousness about health and living sustainably, we have seen a renewed appreciation of cooking, which in turn puts the emphasis back on where the magic happens. This is reflected in restaurants, where open kitchens have become de rigueur, and in what Gilbert calls the "culinary voyeurism" of food media: we can't get enough of cooking on TV and in the press. Just as kitchens are no longer simply food prep spaces, chefs themselves are no longer just the people that make your dinner: they are "personalities", often very famous ones.

A reversion to cooking from scratch—and the interest in the ingredients, process, and culture that surrounds food that comes with it—inevitably has implications for how kitchens look, feel, and function. In the spirit of how the kitchen's role has changed, we often now want to make visible what was previously hidden. We're embracing utility as a design feature, from keeping cookware and produce out on display to bringing the outside in with houseplants, or through the use of raw, sometimes industrial materials for units. In other cases, kitchens have taken on a more decorative aspect, subtly integrating equipment and championing colors, textures, and objects that might once have felt more at home in a traditional reception room. As practical spaces in which we spend more and more time, we naturally want kitchens to work well and look good, to reflect the people who live in them both practically and aesthetically.

And so, this book: a tribute to contemporary kitchens of all shapes and sizes, from the expansive and open plan to built-in or modular arrangements in small, improvised spaces. In these pages, you'll find examples of kitchens put together across a number of countries, on a range of budgets, and for everyone from single solo dwellers to roommates and large families. Some are owned and some are rented, some are temples to cooking while others are refuges, and the people who occupy them have lives and work that demand different things from their kitchen spaces. The starting point is always a source of heat—a stove, an oven, some kind of hearth—and from there the building blocks of the kitchens diverge. I only wish I'd had it as a resource when doing my kitchen.

I got my kitchen in the end, a little room overlooking a sunny garden in a southeast London maisonette. We started by installing a cooker in the chimney breast and, aside from a concrete countertop, kept costs down by using raw materials and embracing an "unfinished" look with plaster, plywood, and bare painted floorboards. A single splash of color comes in the form of some Mexican tiles, and usually a large bowl of lemons awaits a recipe. Most excitingly, I have cookbook shelves and a spice cupboard, a knife magnet and tea towel hooks, so everything that once lived in those boxes now has a home—dubious incense and all.

Mina Holland is a journalist, editor, and author specializing in food, drink, and lifestyle. She is deputy editor of the Guardian's Saturday "Feast" supplement and regularly contributes to various sections of the *Guardian* newspaper. She is the author of two food books, *The Edible Atlas* (Canongate, 2014) and *Mamma* (Orion, 2017) and lives in London.

5

A Pared-Back Galley in Oak and Corian

Design studio Jack Trench made this bespoke kitchen the focal point in the open-plan living and dining area of a handsome Georgian town house in London. "The client's aesthetic is very contemporary, but we were designing for a period architectural space, so the modern kitchen had to allow these elements to breathe," say the designers, who opted for a galley layout and veneered oak cabinetry encased in white Corian to stop the units from clashing with the wooden floor.

"The hob and oven cabinetry has been designed as a cantilevered elevation so that it appears to float gracefully off the ground," they add. An effect that appears all the more impressive due to the extra-deep cupboards, which provide a generous workspace and ample storage. "It's worth noting that you can always customize your countertop size when installing an off-the-shelf kitchen," says the studio. "However, because the high-street kitchen companies work to pre-defined sizes, the cabinetry itself will be set forward at the standard depth no matter the depth of the countertop."

"It's worth noting that you can also *customize* your countertop size when installing an off-the-shelf kitchen"

→ *This bespoke kitchen features a galley layout and veneered oak cabinetry encased in white Corian. "The hob and oven units have been designed as a cantilevered elevation so that it appears to float gracefully off the ground," say its designers.*

→ *All of Nordiska Kök's kitchens are crafted from scratch in its Gothenburg workshop. A focus on timelessness and durability underpins everything it designs, as does a desire to "leave the lightest possible touch on world resources."*

The Effortless Route to Enviable Nordic Style

Swedish brand Nordiska Kök draws on a long legacy of Scandinavian design to create its tailor-made kitchens. Its aim is to create spaces where "the coffee tastes better and where a dinner quickly turns into a party," says the company, which produces its designs in its Gothenburg workshop.

"Our kitchens are built to last for years, and to leave the lightest possible footprint on world resources," says the brand. Whether in dark oak or pale ash, many of its projects showcase the beauty of raw wood, pairing it with minimalist cabinetry and hidden handles. Complementary materials might include terrazzo, for a touch of old-world glamour, or limestone sourced from Gotland or Kinnekulle. "A fitted kitchen should not be complicated or expensive. That's why we make it simple," say Nordiska Kök, who will guide you through the design process and produce your new kitchen in as little as four to six weeks. The units will then arrive in pre-mounted frames, with drawers and fronts, ready for installation.

→ *Many of its projects showcase the beauty of raw wood, pairing the natural warmth of timber with minimalist cabinetry and hidden handles.*

→ Warm, rustic and contemporary, this kitchen features a line of units made from dark oak, which have been topped with a steel surface. The pale gray central island lightens the look, the countertop of which is made from Gotland limestone.

→ Uno Form's timeless C-Series kitchen was designed in 1968 and looks as fresh today as it did then.

Danish Design That Has Stood the Test of Time

Uno Form started out in 1968 when founder Arne Munch designed the company's first kitchen at his home in Lyngby. "Innovative and uncompromising Danish kitchen design" is how the brand describes its work, which focuses on traditional joinery undertaken by skilled craftspeople. When first launched, Uno Form offered a radical alternative to the kitchens available at the time, which allowed little in the way of freedom or originality when it came to layout.

Munch's solution was a simple cube-shaped module, the C-Series, which could be configured in infinite permutations. He was inspired by cabinetry used elsewhere in the home and insisted on incorporating this same design-led aesthetic into his kitchen, devising the characteristic handle-free slotted fronts responsible for turning the Uno Form kitchen into a Danish design classic. "Many Uno Form kitchens produced back in the 1960s and 70s are fully functional to this day," says the brand. "Lots have changed owners over the years, some several times." A testament to the enduring power of good design.

→ *Uno Form offered a radical alternative to the kitchens available at the time of its launch, as there was then little freedom when it came to layout. The cube-shaped module can be configured in different permutations and comes in a variety of finishes.*

→ *Here, pale timber base units have been used to balance out the dark gray cabinetry, helping to lift the space. The floating design of the base cabinets is also great for compact kitchens, as it contributes to a sense of spaciousness.*

Brimful of *Originality* and Focused on Family

Discover a slick and resilient redesign that honors this home's rich history

Jonathan Richards

→ *Undaunted by the awkward triangular floor plan, owner and architect Jonathan Richards set about redesigning this historic property in a bid to unveil the character of the original building and remodel the interior for his family.*

Built in 1890, this home in Darlinghurst, Sydney, was once a two-story house with its own stable. Over the years, the building evolved with many different uses and functions, and now consists of three levels, the top two of which are a single residence. Faced with an awkward triangular floor plan, owner-architect Jonathan Richards's intent was to unveil the character of the original building and remodel the interior for his family.

"In an area like Darlinghurst, which is characterized by terrace houses, this building started like no other and has continued to become even more unusual over time," says Richards, founder of his own architecture and design practice, Richards Stanisich. "We saw enormous character in the history and wanted the new design to settle in effortlessly beside the old bones." The kitchen was designed as part of the larger renovation of the entire house; the floor plan was reworked and the space reconfigured. "The building is 130 years old, with many old quirks and idiosyncrasies. We loved that about it and wanted to make sure its charm was very much intact when we finished," he adds. Designed for a family of four, the new kitchen is in constant use, so it needed to be hardwearing. As for the aesthetic, "The style is my style," says Richards of the space, which features teal-stained cabinets, gray dolomite countertops, and sea-blue walls. "I love the green color and I enjoy spaces that feel very easy and livable." The architect admits that achieving the paint finish on the cabinetry was a challenge. "I wanted the timber grain and the right color. Getting both took quite a few finish samples and prototypes by the builder. The paint had to be thin enough to reveal the grain

→ *Cupboards line the lower half of the kitchen, but the walls are free of cabinets. Instead, Richards opted for open shelves with fluted-glass sliding doors.*

but tough enough to withstand heavy use." Cabinetry is reserved for the lower half of the kitchen as the family disliked the idea of having cupboards hung above. Instead, they opted for open shelves for pantry goods and left a few blank spaces to allow artwork to be incorporated into the design. As the kitchen also doubles as the dining room, Richards Stanisich created a built-in banquette seat in tan leather that wraps around a custom oak table. "We needed to maximize space so that the dining table would fit as many people as possible and the kitchen still functioned perfectly," says Richards, who also chose to close off a door to the external courtyard and replace it with windows above the banquette.

The finished space is an unconventional yet cohesive fusion of elements that honors the property's idiosyncratic feel. "This building contains generations of changes to an already unusual typology. Our design deliberately makes it a little unclear what is new and what's old and what, if anything, was original," Richards explains. "The design has a few elements that reflect on an older style—like the fluted glass sliding doors and the stained timber—but by breaking down the traditional kitchen, it feels very contemporary." ▪

"We saw enormous character and wanted the new design to settle in effortlessly beside the old bones"

→ *Achieving the paint effect on the teal-colored cabinetry was no easy feat. It had to be thin enough to show the grain and thick enough for daily use. The result works beautifully with the Dolomite worktops and dark walls.*

Drawing on a Heritage of Craftsmanship

Belgian brand Obumex has been creating luxurious custom-made kitchens for the past 60 years, partnering with architects such as John Pawson and Joseph Dirand, and designer Grégoire de Lafforest, for some of its concepts. The family-run company was founded by Eli Ostyn, growing from a joinery firm into a specialist kitchen and furniture designer that works with 120 crafts-people to execute its projects. Most of its designs are totally bespoke, bar the collaborations with Pawson and Dirand: concept kitchens that can be adapted to suit your space and needs. Dirand's creation harnesses the timeless beauty of Paonazzetto marble and patinaed bronze. As for de Lafforest, he drew inspiration from libraries to design a timber kitchen that plays with ideas of display and concealment. "It was a privilege to cooperate with specialist craftsmen who are real experts in their jobs," said the French designer. "Thanks to their expertise, I was able to realize a kitchen idea that is incomparable in the field of custom work."

→ *Collaborating with leading designers and architects helps this 60-year-old brand to keep producing work that's fresh and current. This kitchen was designed by Grégoire de Lafforest, who looked to library design for inspiration.*

"It was a privilege to cooperate with *specialist craftsmen* who are real experts in their jobs"

→ *Belgian architect Glenn Sestig designed this Obumex kitchen, which serves as both a room divider and a bar. Made from natural stone and travertine titanium, it's intended for luxe city apartments, where the kitchen forms a sculptural statement.*

→ *"Most contemporary kitchen designs are dominated by horizontal lines. We break through this cliché with a vertical volume, a strong architectural statement. A fully equipped cocktail cabinet is hidden here," says Sestig.*

Most of the designs are totally bespoke *concept kitchens* that can be adapted to suit your space and needs

→ *Statement marbles feature in much of Obumex's work, such as in this renovated city home (below), which features a striking island with integrated bench and matching marble dining table.*

A Matter of *Materials*

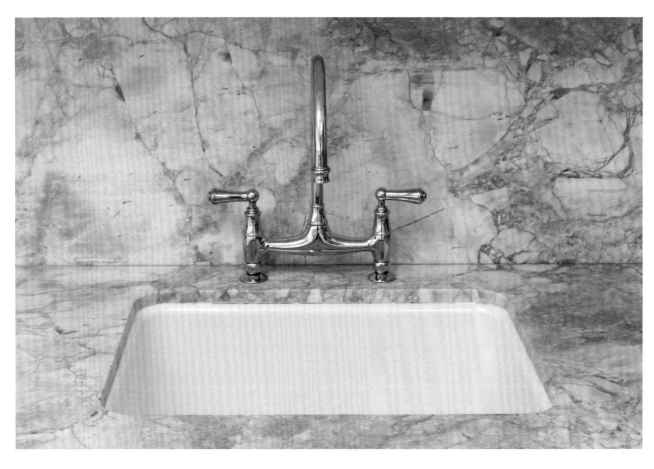

From reclaimed wood
to polished stone, the
right materials and fixtures
can upscale even the
simplest of schemes

The Materials

Anna-Tina Schaal and her husband, Andreas, used reclaimed wood to clad the sides of the island counter in their Cape Town kitchen. The rugged timber had been salvaged from the house during the renovation work and serves to offset the glossy metro tiles and steel countertop.

"Inspiration comes first," says interior stylist and creative director Alex Kristal when asked about how to approach designing a new kitchen. The former decorating editor of British *Elle Decoration* recommends spending a good deal of time collating images from various sources—whether from magazines, design blogs, or Pinterest—to define your aesthetic. The next step is to make that look work for your budget and your lifestyle.

"Whatever style you aspire to can be translated into something more affordable," says Kristal, but that's not the only constraining factor. "Functionality is paramount," she adds. "You see images of kitchens that look beautiful but they're completely unsuitable →

A penchant for 1960s design inspired the graphic, grid-like tiled countertops that Etica Studio installed in this house in Perth, Western Australia, which have been paired with a concrete backdrop and plywood cabinetry. The tiled backsplash has been built out from the wall to create a shelf for storage and display.

Interior architect Anthi Grapsa designed this utility room, which is brand new but looks years old thanks to her expert eye for salvaging. Reclaimed Welsh slate roof tiles provide a hardy backsplash behind the sink, while an old paint-splattered iroko wood board serves as a countertop.

Architects Catrina Stewart and Hugh McEwen of Office S&M used a bold and varied material palette to define different spaces in this west London home. In the kitchen, bright yellow grout was used to set the pale pink herringbone tiles, a continuation of a color theme used elsewhere in the house.

for daily use, and that's often down to the material choices." For example, if you love the look of marble but want to use it on a countertop, you might be wise to consider a composite stone that looks just as good but is more durable, less porous, and potentially cheaper. "It's really about understanding how your chosen materials will react, both initially and over time," she says.

In addition to durability, your material palette will affect how your kitchen weathers passing trends too. Natural materials rarely date and are an easy way to liven up a minimalist scheme. Salvaged elements bring their own brand of timelessness and can be an affordable way to create a kitchen with a huge amount of character. "Be sure to source reclaimed timber and fittings from a reputable dealer," cautions Kristal. "And remember that while you might save money on materials, installing salvaged pieces can sometimes be a costly process." If budget is a concern, you can't beat plywood for versatility at a good price. "If you pick the right grade, it's incredibly strong. It can be easily colored and customized, and can be used to build almost anything," she affirms. She also recommends Valchromat, an easy-to-work-with MDF substitute that comes →

Interior designer Victoria Maria used Marmoreal for the countertop, backsplash, and floor of this Brussels kitchen. Available in two colorways, the engineered marble-and-resin terrazzo was developed specifically for architectural use by Dzek in collaboration with designer Max Lamb.

These countertops might look like they are crafted from rugged concrete, but they are in fact made from hardwearing quartz—one of nature's hardest minerals—by Caesarstone. Unlike concrete, these countertops are naturally non-porous, negating the need for sealing or waxing.

Part of Caesarstone's Metropolitan Collection, this Cloudburst Concrete countertop is made from 93 percent natural quartz, organic pigments, and enhanced polymer resins. Scratch, chip, and impact resistant, this durable surface is anti-microbial and resistant to staining.

The owners of this kitchen approached Belgian design studio Dialect after spotting its work in a fashion boutique in Antwerp. The pink resin floor of the store provided the inspiration for the design, which features handle-free MDF cabinets in rose-colored lacquer topped with work surfaces of pink granite.

pre-colored in a range of different shades. While Kristal's own design preferences tend to prioritize simplicity, she notes that in general, people are becoming more experimental with their kitchen interiors, happily mixing materials and introducing accents of color and pattern. "I think people are starting to get a bit more playful, particularly with tiles," she says. "And not just with the designs themselves, but how they're used within the space."

Whatever materials you choose, Kristal believes that practicality is the key to a kitchen that is as enjoyable to live with as it to look at. "It's worth considering that almost half the time spent in the kitchen involves cleaning it, so if you've got lots of grooves, gaps, and cracks between the various elements, it makes the task more arduous." Investing in the parts that get the most wear and tear is another recommendation, whether that's brassware, cabinet handles, or surfaces. "It's the most-used room in the house, after all," she says. "And a few high-end fixtures can totally transform a high-street kitchen." ▪

"I gathered images over many years and homed in on the materials that I liked most," says photographic director and creative producer Flora Bathurst of her "bullet-proof modern-classic" kitchen, which features reclaimed cabinetry from a school science lab, concrete countertops, and a brass backsplash.

A Blank Slate

From slabs of quartz to recycled glass, choose the right materials to help set the tone for all of your kitchen exploits

The kitchen is the hub of the home, and gets a huge amount of traffic, so finding the right brands and suppliers is critical: their wares need to be able to stand the test of time.

From crisp, freshly quarried slate to aged hardwood with a well-loved patina, selecting the right set of materials for a kitchen should never be an afterthought. Instead, those countertops, backsplashes, and tiles provide a blueprint for your interior. Italian design collective *Mutina* focuses on thoughtfully crafted ceramics for walls and floors that will weather a life lived well. They offer sophisticated tiles with natural glazes in an array of soft-spoken colors that let your furnishings and fixtures do the talking. The collections are tied together by muted palettes—burnt orange, powdery emerald, and many, many shades of grey. Led by a team of legendary interior designers, including German industrial designer Konstantin Grcic, Mutina is known for its industrious innovations.

Dzek creates immaculate designer architectural surfaces by combining quality materials with tried-and-true workmanship for its projects. Founded by leading London-based design talent Brent Dzekciorius, the company works with slabs of composite that are measured and cut into countertops, tiled flooring, and even accent walls. Peppered with colorful cross-cut chips and stones, Dzek's terrazzo represents a more outspoken pedigree in interior design, which dates back to Dzekciorius's passion for the Bauhaus school's mastery in combining technology, art, and craftsmanship. California brand *Vetrazzo* is cut from the same cloth: here, recycled glass is grafted into each composite to create dazzling mosaics that range from subdued neutrals to bright pops of color, bold blues, greens, and reds of tumbled sea glass.

Belgium's *Hullebusch* also excels at bringing the ample beauty of the great outdoors inside. Natural stones are cut into tables, chairs, countertops, and columns with a patient eye for the splendor of each rock's grain, lines, and bands. Denmark's *Furnipart* follows a similar thread: many of its door and cabinet handles are crafted from leather, cast iron, and brass with a lightly textured finish that would pair perfectly with an aged hardwood floor or exposed brick accent wall. *Caesarstone*

focuses on premium quartz slabs, rich with organic waves and crests of color beneath their smooth surfaces. There's a beauty in these so-called imperfections: though the rich, rustic textures may seem like a small detail, they have an immeasurable impact when tying together a room. For some, however, building a kitchen that will last a lifetime means looking to the future. Germany's *Dornbracht* offers fixtures with digital controls, and *41zero42* designs each collection of tiles with a respect for the past and an eye on what the future of contemporary aesthetics might hold. As the possibilities are endless, designing a kitchen may seem daunting. Start by choosing the right materials to set the mood and palette for a kitchen.

Still looking for more inspiration? Browse a full index of designers, brands, and suppliers at the back of the book.

A London Extension That Defies Convention

"This project was about making something extraordinary out of the very ordinary," say Luke McLaren and Robert Excell of architecture and interiors practice McLaren Excell, who were approached to extend and refurbish a Victorian terraced house in west London for a growing family. While the brief was somewhat conventional, the client was keen to avoid the typical "planning-friendly aesthetics" of a London terraced house extension. "From the outset, discussions centered around the use of concrete," explain the architects, who used the material for floors, walls, and a monolithic central island. "We chose it mainly for its aesthetic qualities, but also the opportunity to build in high thermal mass and develop free-form structures," they add. Naturally, this influenced all other material choices too, from the extension's Corten steel façade to the interior joinery made from gray elm, chosen to create a contrasting richness that counterbalances the swathes of cool, smooth concrete.

→ The kitchen of this old Mallorcan town house is completely concealed within its walls, a decision made by Isla Architects to enhance the effect of the room's vaulted ceiling. The modern dining table makes a vibrant centerpiece.

Mediterranean Modern in a Traditional Town House

Located in the coastal village of Banyalbufar in Mallorca, this old town house, has been renovated by Isla Architects, who were tasked with restoring the entire home as well as rearranging the interiors. The first job was to remove all non-original aspects in order to enhance the character of the house, before adding contemporary elements. "The balance between modern and old, sleek and rustic, brings a new life to the house," say the architects, who cleverly concealed the kitchen within the walls of the building to enhance the effect of the room's vaulted ceiling. Existing niches were enlarged to accommodate appliances such as a fridge, oven, and washing machine, and storage for tableware, utensils, and food. The stove was placed below the window so the owners could look out over the Mediterranean Sea when cooking. All materials were sourced locally, as was the tinted-concrete sink by Huguet, chosen to represent the traditional Mallorcan stone sink, while the tap was forged from a simple piece of brass pipe.

"The balance between modern and old, sleek and rustic, brings *a new life* to the house"

→ *All materials were sourced locally, as was the tinted-concrete sink by Huguet, chosen to represent the traditional Mallorcan stone sink.*

Elegant Materials and a Compact Scheme

The refurbishment of this small duplex apartment in Brussels was undertaken by Dries Otten, a design studio based in Antwerp. A great example of an imaginatively compact interior, the flat combines a kitchen, dining room, and living area within just 35 m² (377 ft²). The main focus was to integrate the three spaces "We didn't want the kitchen to look too much like a kitchen," explains the studio, "so we used classic materials such as American walnut veneer and terrazzo, and created the round island as an abstract room divider." The oven is hidden inside the island, while above is a custom cooker hood with the same diameter. When Dries Otten started work on the space, it was a blank canvas, but one with a little character due to the wooden floors and double-height windows. "We chose to use light colors to keep the space feeling as fresh as possible," the designers add, referencing the soft green lacquer applied to the sandblasted pine-veneer cabinetry and the shelves made of pale terrazzo.

→ Carpenter Pär, pictured with his two children, Ebbe and Iris, in the kitchen that he installed and customized. Pär and his wife, Lovisa, designed the kitchen themselves, and were inspired by designs from the 1940s and 50s.

Pretty in Pink with a Monochrome Edge

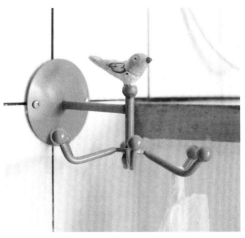

When resourceful Swedish couple Pär and Lovisa started planning their new kitchen, it was the Smeg fridge that set the color scheme. They had never intended to go for pink, but once the fridge was in, it seemed like the obvious choice. The couple live in a 1930s apartment in Malmö with their children, Ebbe and Iris, and wanted a design that referenced the 1940s and 50s, and a pastel scheme that felt contemporary. The kitchen itself was found on the internet—free, if disassembled. Luckily, Pär is a carpenter so he knows a thing or two about DIY. After installing the frame, they replaced the doors and found the vintage cabinet handles at a building preservation store. Pär molded the concrete countertop himself and used dark grout between the tiles to give the pink scheme a bit of an edge. A quirky picture by illustrator Anna Sonesson and fun festoon lighting emphasize the black-and-white backdrop.

"Pär used dark grout between the tiles to give *the pink scheme* a bit of an edge"

→ *Pär and Lovisa found their secondhand kitchen for free on the internet. The couple decided to have the doors spray-painted pink, they then chose graphic, monochrome touches and a concrete countertop to toughen up the scheme.*

A Belgian Studio's Fresh Take on Rose

The owners of this pink kitchen approached Belgian design studio Atelier Dialect after spotting its work in a minimalist fashion boutique in Antwerp. Co-founder Pierric De Coster trained as an architect, while his partner, Jonas Blondeel, is "a man of action," focusing on the materials and technical parts of the project. "Both our creative languages are essential to the end stresult," says the duo. "We see the entire process as an opportunity to create a durable, honest, and universal design."

The pink resin floor of the Antwerp store provided both the impetus and the inspiration for this kitchen, which features handle-free MDF cabinets in rose-colored lacquer. In the center, an angular, asymmetrical island has been ergonomically designed to make efficient use of the small space, while mirrored panels have been added throughout to create new and interesting angles and views. Worktops crafted from pink granite complement the units, while a white Smeg hob and Vola tap keep the look light and fresh.

→ *The curvaceous kitchen that Colombo and Serboli Architecture designed for this centuries-old building features a coral-colored volume that cleverly conceals a separate cloakroom. Brass accents have been implemented throughout, and surfaces are clad in pink terrazzo-like quartz.*

Coral and Curves Update an Ancient Apartment

This apartment is located in one of the oldest neighborhoods of Barcelona, in a building that dates back to the thirteenth century. Colombo and Serboli Architecture was asked to completely transform the old property into a vibrant home for a young Italian woman who works in fashion. The new arrangement aimed to restore and enhance the grand proportions of the centuries-old building, which features lofty vaulted ceilings, large windows, and thick walls.

False ceilings were removed to expose the Catalan vaults and ceiling beams, which were all painted white to brighten the space. The new, open kitchen is a seamless composition of curves, from the central island to the custom dining table and the coral-colored structure that cleverly conceals a separate cloakroom. Brass accents can be seen throughout, including the vintage handles that have been fitted to the warm-gray-painted cabinets. All surfaces, including the backsplash, are clad in a pink terrazzo-like quartz—a perfect match for the statement coral volume that presides over the space.

The Ultimate Hack for Your IKEA Cabinets

"IKEA is second to none when it comes to creating high-quality kitchen modules at very reasonable prices," say Jeppe Christensen and Michael Andersen, founders of Danish brand Reform. It has specialized in customizing the Swedish retailer's off-the-shelf kitchens with upscale cabinetry since the pair spotted a gap in the market for affordable custom solutions.

They set about collaborating with internationally acclaimed architects, such as BIG, Henning Larsen, and Norm, to bring great design to the masses. "For many people, the heart of the home is the kitchen," says Christensen, "but this is a room that's often overlooked ... with design as an afterthought. Reform wants to change this."

Once you have acquired your IKEA cabinets, all you need to do is select fronts and countertops from Reform's architect-designed range to customize your space. From timeless options, like the 1960s-inspired Basis model, to Norm's dramatic smoked oak range, there is a wealth of contemporary designs to choose from.

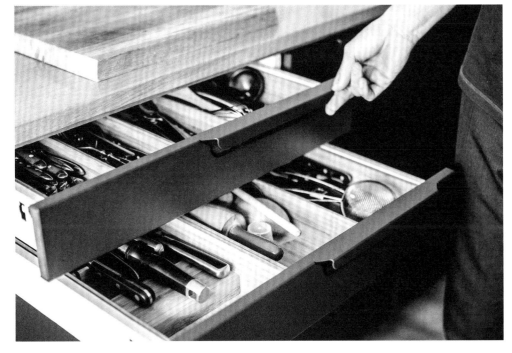

For many people, the *heart of the home* is the kitchen, but its design is often an afterthought

→ *The brand created this gleaming kitchen out of brass for the headquarters of Danish fashion designer Stine Goya. The model is a bespoke version of Reform's Chelsea design, a collaboration with designer Christina Meyer Bengtsson.*

→ Bengtsson's original design was a mix of mauve, gray, and brass fronts; Goya's customized model has cupboards and side panels clad entirely in brass, brass handles, and a black laminate countertop.

→ *The Basis model was Reform's first design and is based on 1960s architect kitchens. It comes in three different styles: painted, linoleum, and veneer, all of which are characterized by the milled-in round handle.*

→ "We love to combine the Basis design with a countertop in linoleum," says Reform. It also recommends a solid wood countertop, which comes in either natural oak or smoked oak—each choice a great complement to the signature oak handle.

Jailmake

Finding the Flow Between Kitchen and Garden

Located in Peckham, London, this 1960s home underwent a "simple, utilitarian redesign" at the hands of local studio Jailmake, who overhauled the kitchen and dining areas to improve the flow and make more of the outdoor space. "The renovation keeps in touch with the roots of the building, linking the living space to the garden without turning its back on the minimalist style of the era," says designer Jamie Elliott.

The new kitchen is built from a sycamore frame that was handmade to fit the space and that features more than six meters of continuous grain from a single tree. The proportions allowed for the seamless integration of appliances, while visual simplicity was retained with considered touches, such as hidden runners and magnetic socket covers.

Complementing and contrasting materials have been balanced throughout, with the organic tones of the continuous cork floor helping to offset the kitchen's graphic quality. Outside, the redesigned garden continues the textural and contemporary theme.

Visual simplicity was retained with *considered touches*, such as hidden runners and magnetic socket covers

→ *Jailmake overhauled the kitchen and dining areas of this 1960s home with a new layout that improves the flow and makes more of the garden. Complementing and contrasting materials combine, while cork flooring offsets the kitchen's graphic quality.*

A Textural Kitchen with a Sense of *Calm*

Earthy materials combine with uncluttered designs in the impressively organized kitchen of this restaurateur couple

Laura Harper-Hinton

→ *"Natural, calm, and warm," is how Harper-Hinton describes this space. Light- and dark-stained oak cabinets are complemented by pale stone work surfaces, while textural, woven pieces contribute to the modern-rustic mix.*

"I came up with this concept based on the fact that my last kitchen was very eclectic and busy, with lots of vintage pieces and everything on display," says Laura Harper-Hinton of the kitchen in her west London home. "This time, with two little boys in the mix, I wanted to create something that had clean lines and a sense of calm." The co-founder and creative director of London's Caravan restaurants designed the kitchen herself and wanted to make sure that every item had a home so they could be put away easily at the end of a busy day.

The original kitchen was tired and dated, so Harper-Hinton and her partner, Chris Ammerman, gutted the space and started again from scratch. "Because we work in the restaurant industry, we love entertaining, so I wanted to have enough room for a 14-person dining table and big cooking and living area." The couple extended to the party wall and built out into the garden as well to create a large kitchen, dining, and living space. They dug down into the ground to create extra ceiling height, helping to add to the kitchen's spacious feel. "At one point, we thought we were going to have to underpin the whole ground floor to achieve this," she says. "Luckily, we didn't!"

They also decided to open up the entire floor with a wide central flow through from the living room: "This meant we had to install some pretty serious steel beams." Now, sliding glass-paneled timber doors mark the entrance to the new kitchen, which is set down a level from the living space. They also built a vast skylight into the ceiling above the central island, which, alongside the glass doors to the garden, helps fill the room

→ Plants line the steps leading to the kitchen, which is set down a level from the living space to increase the height of the room.

with light. As for the aesthetic, "natural, calm, and warm" is how Harper-Hinton describes it. A wealth of organic, earthy materials combine in the uncluttered design, such as the light- and dark-stained oak cabinets topped with stone work surfaces. Clay plaster—on the wall behind the dining table and above the cookline—adds a certain softness, as do an array of textural, woven pieces. The large antique cupboard, found at a vintage shop in Brighton, is a traditional touch that fits happily into the modern-rustic mix.

True to brief, the space is incredibly organized, with floor-to-ceiling cupboards holding anything that does not need to be on display. "I have a great pantry," she says. "It's where all my jars of ferments, grains, pulses, and spices live, and can be easily tidied away to." Small appliances, such as the coffee machine, are hidden behind closed doors, and much thought went into the flow of the kitchen to ensure an ergonomic design. Now, the space works for the whole family, whether entertaining friends or helping the children with their homework. "I spent a long time working on this and there is nothing I would change. Flow is really important—it makes cooking so joyful." ▬

→ *"We work in the restaurant industry and love entertaining, so I wanted to have enough room for a 14-person dining table and big cooking and living area," says Harper-Hinton.*

"I wanted to make sure every item could be put away easily at the end of a busy day"

→ *Clay plaster—on the wall behind the dining table and above the cooking line—softens the sleek interior. "I wanted to create somewhere that had clean lines and a sense of calm," Harper-Hinton adds.*

The Ultimate in Highly Customizable Luxury

"A movement towards a broader, more personal approach to kitchen design" is how Lanserring describes Tradescant, a bespoke collection that forms "the basis of an eclectic kitchen environment." Drawing from historical references and modern-living trends, Tradescant is crafted from an incredible range of materials. Think woven gold mesh; six different timbers; a selection of polished, leathered, and honed natural stones; and embossed leather finishes.

The Oilcloth Island is made from polished metal and veined natural stone, while the sink pairs stone and metal to recreate the traditional butler model. Inspired by the Victorian-era kitchen, the Scullery Table can be customized with built-in scales or hand-blown crystal spice drawers, while the Vitrine glass storage cupboard is a contemporary take on a sixteenth-century cabinet of curiosities. As with all good design, detail is everything—that is why you will find timber drawers carved to fit your possessions and secret wall hooks that fold out of the backsplash.

Drawing from historical references and modern–living trends, Tradescant is crafted from an *incredible range* of materials

→ *London-based brand Lanserring's unique designs include the Oilcloth Island, crafted from polished metal and veined natural stone, and the Victorian-inspired Scullery Table, to which you can add features such as built-in scales or hand-blown crystal spice drawers.*

Artisan Interiors for a Waterside Abode

Set on the waterfront in Sydney's Palm Beach, this elegant holiday villa was overhauled by local design firm Alexander & Co. The redesign prioritized a handmade aesthetic, so materials, fittings, finishes, and lighting were chosen to convey an artisanal feel. Pared-back furniture and a subdued palette allow the textural qualities of the interior to shine, as well as the ocean views.

The kitchen forms part of an open-plan living space that "spills out" into the garden, according to its designers—perfect for entertaining the friends and family that regularly come to stay. "With the focus on refined design details, a high level of craftsmanship was required," say Alexander & Co, referencing elements such as the solid walnut sideboard and the Carrara marble island, which features a brass gooseneck tap from The English Tapware Company. Thule stools from Great Dane Furniture flank the breakfast bar, their sleek design an unexpected match for the classic lines of the heavy marble counter.

Alexander & Co

→ *At the center of this kitchen by Alexander & Co is a huge Carrara marble island, which perfectly complements the pale cabinetry. Dark walnut wood and brass add warmth, as well as contributing to the space's artisan feel.*

The Details Make *the Difference*

From a lick of paint to the perfect piece of art, little updates can have a big impact on any space—and the kitchen is no exception

Consider bringing in color through both functional and decorative items. "I love open shelving in a kitchen but am of the opinion that day-to-day items should occupy easy-to-reach spots for the best use of space," says interior designer Tiffany Duggan.

The Details

"We're noticing a real shift away from super-sleek kitchens," says interior designer Tiffany Duggan, founder of London-based firm Studio Duggan. "The key to a kitchen that people want to spend time in is to create a space that tells their story, filled with their favorite things." Duggan's own kitchen, artfully lit and adorned with pictures, textiles, glassware, and ceramics, is the kind of place where you would happily while away a few hours. The designer prefers both kitchens and bathrooms to feel lived in and well decorated, rather than cold or sterile, and she thinks others are following suit. "More and more, kitchens are turning into living spaces, so they need to be warm, comforting, and unified with the rest of the house," she explains. →

Designed to perch on the edge of your sink, this colorful cat sponge is part of a range of imaginative cleaning products by Danish brand Hay. Other fun finds include stripy tawashi scrubbers and heart-shaped scourers with smiley faces.

Updating your space could be as easy as bringing in some textiles or a new lighting scheme. In this kitchen by Oslo-based Dagny Fargestudio, a low-hanging pendant light stands out against the textural plaster used on the walls, while a colorful rug warms up the wooden floor and green cabinetry.

The owners of this 1950s-inspired kitchen bought the units secondhand and installed new doors, which they had painted pastel pink. Statement artwork provides a focal point, while everyday items add further character. "Cookbooks, ceramics, potted herbs ... they can all be left out on display," says Duggan.

Much like any other space in your home, adding a little personality does not need to be a feat of design. If you have hand-painted or bare timber units, refreshing the room with a new color palette is a relatively easy option. Alternatively, a new lick of paint on the walls or woodwork can make a big difference, as can retiling your backsplash. "I love to use color on kitchen cabinets, but it can be a big commitment," acknowledges Duggan. "Tiles are a much less overwhelming way to bring in new shades or patterns. A beautiful handmade tile can add heaps of character."

If tiling is still a step too far, the designer recommends using crockery and glassware to brighten up your space—an ideal option if you have open shelving or glass-fronted cupboards. "Proceed with caution" is her caveat: "I love open shelving in a kitchen but am of the opinion that day-to-day items should occupy easy-to-reach spots for the best use of space. Glasses, jugs, mugs, and bowls look great on a kitchen shelf but will gather dust if only there for display."

Other quick fixes include artwork, lampshades, and textiles, all of which can help to balance out hard surfaces and soften a kitchen's utilitarian feel. "Colored, pre-distressed leathers are perfect for →

"You can't beat plants for a really quick, inexpensive decorating solution. It may sound obvious, but they go a long way if you're trying to add a little life to a space." Pictures and prints are another easy update—here they have been used to frame a vintage bar trolley, which doubles as a display surface.

Hand-painted or bare timber units are relatively easy to update with a fresh lick of paint. Interior design studio Jersey Ice Cream Co used Seaworthy by Sherwin-Williams to define this compact kitchen—the perfect backdrop for brass accents, such as handles, taps, and lighting.

If you prefer a neutral palette, look to contrasting shades, shapes, and textures to create subtle depth and interest within a monochrome scheme. Wooden pieces are a surefire way to make a contemporary kitchen feel homelier, as are carefully chosen vintage finds.

As William Morris famously said: "Have nothing in your house that you do not know to be useful or believe to be beautiful." Seeking out everyday objects that are well designed and a pleasure to look at, such as this stainless-steel water kettle by Hay, negates the need for excess decorative clutter.

busy spaces as they just get better with age," she advises. "There are also some remarkable outdoor fabrics around these days, which are perfect for kitchen use."

Another go-to is lighting, integral to the success of any well-decorated room. "It's particularly important to have both task and mood lighting so you can adapt your space for cooking and dining, especially if your main table is in the kitchen," says Duggan, who recommends integrating wall lights, pendants, and table lamps into your scheme, as well as fitting dimmer switches to spotlights to help control the mood.

Armed with this advice, even the most minimal of kitchens can be transformed into a homely and welcoming environment, whether you rent or own your home. "It can be as simple as a new lamp, a piece of art, or a patterned floor rug," says Duggan. "And for a really quick, inexpensive solution, you can't beat plants and herbs. It may sound obvious, but they go a long way if you're trying to add a little life to a space." ▬

"More and more, kitchens are turning into living spaces, so they need to be warm, comforting, and unified with the rest of the house," says Duggan. Here, in this kitchen by Lanserring, a slim shelf is the perfect place to display art and objects, while task lighting is as elegant as it is practical.

Transform Your Kitchen

Creating a kitchen as unique as you are is all about the details. Here's where to hunt for unique pieces to personalize your space

Bringing the subtle warmth and textures of nature into your kitchen comes easily to design studios and brands in the Nordic region, where natural elements are part of the local design DNA.

Iconic Finnish brand *Marimekko* creates colorful, rounded natural prints that feature on everything from textiles (think curtains, tea towels, cushions, and beyond) to kitchenware, with prints that look as modern today as they did in the 1950s, under the eye of visionary designer and co-founder Armi Ratia. If you had

to pick just one place to visit to find the best of contemporary Scandinavian design, Copenhagen is the clear winner. At the forefront is *Hay,* where creative directors and Danish power couple Mette and Rolf Hay have been collaborating with leading global designers to create instant classics that are stocked at places like the MoMA in New York City. In 2017, Mette launched the Hay Kitchen Market, which works with international and local talent, like forward-thinking Danish chef Frederik Bille Brahe, to transform kitchen basics into

colorful, covetable essentials. Characteristic of the new vanguard of Scandinavian design are three more Copenhagen-based brands, *Stilleben*, *Ferm Living*, and *Paper Collective*. Whether it's an expertly curated collection of ceramics at Stilleben, or Ferm Living's quirky detailing, like art deco hooks and richly knitted tea towels, products manage to feel one of a kind. When it comes to decorating your walls, Paper Collective collaborates with the best of the Scandinavian creative scene, selling everything from a selection of abstract architectural photography chosen by Norm Architects to richly detailed floral still life images shot by local fashion talent. Storing your kitchenware and displaying artwork doesn't have to be dull with *String Furniture*'s cult shelving units that turn Swedish functionality into an art form, with its industrial-chic units that make a statement simply by refusing to hide everything away in a cupboard. If you are looking to inject a little more maximalism rather than minimalism into your kitchen detailing, look to the Italians rather than the Scandinavians. *Alessi* is a household name for good reason, having single-handedly developed more kitchen classics than any other brand can lay claim to—think of Philippe Starck's spiderlike Juicy Salif citrus squeezer or Alessi's sculptural stainless-steel fruit bowls. Sometimes it's the act of stumbling upon a new one-off

treasure that makes it priceless, but in the age of online marketplaces like *1stdibs* and *Etsy*, there is no reason to be stuck rummaging through the cast-offs of local grannies at the flea market. If price is not an object, then American interior design marketplace 1stdibs is your go-to. Founder Michael Bruno was inspired to bring authentic European antiques and twentieth century design to an affluent audience, and today 1stdibs is a success story for its vast global reach that caters to the one percent. But if finding a unique handcrafted kitchen clock at a craft fair is more your idea of a good find than antique gold candlesticks, look to Etsy. Aiming primarily at a millennial audience, creative young craftspeople from around the world have created a bustling marketplace and community that doesn't feel miles away from your local flea market.

If you're looking for more inspiration in sourcing details for your kitchen and the rest of your home, refer to the index at the back of the book for a full selection of brands and design studios.

Durable Kitchens in a Rainbow of Shades

"The ideal kitchen is a living room and workshop at the same time," says German brand Popstahl, whose colorful kitchens are the ultimate low-maintenance option. Made in Austria from powder-coated steel, the designs are incredibly hard-wearing as well as asthetically pleasing.

The concept was inspired by the work of Otl Aicher, a German graphic designer known for the pictograms he produced for the 1972 Olympic Games in Munich (interestingly, he also published a kitchen design book in 1982, which pioneered the merging of kitchens with living spaces). "On the one hand, a kitchen should be functional and practical, so everyday tasks can be done quickly and easily," says Popstahl. "On the other, it has to be a place to feel good."

Whether you need a generous kitchen or a more compact model, like the Kochtisch cooking table, Popstahls designs can be produced in virtually any hue. Stick to one shade or mix it up, and choose from additional materials—such as steel, wood, or concrete—to finish the look.

→ *The zesty yellow color of this steel kitchen was achieved by a powder-coating technique, which Popstahl have perfected. The kitchens can be produced in almost any shade. Stick to one color throughout, mix contrasting hues, or combine complementing tonal shades.*

"A kitchen should be *functional* and *practical*, so everyday tasks can be done quickly and easily"

→ *The incredibly durable designs can also be combined with other materials,*
such as wood, concrete, or plain steel so you can customize the kitchen to suit your space.

Clean and Considered Space–Saving Design

Built on a narrow plot on a small street in Montreal, this four-story residence is the work of Canadian studio La Shed. Due to the small square area of each floor, the living spaces had to be located over two levels, with a kitchen and dining room facing the garden, and a mezzanine living room perched above. Saving space was a key factor in the design, so the kitchen features a compact and highly functional layout. Crisp white cabinets appear to blend in with the walls and are set just below the ceiling to allow light to pass through the space. These also serve as a partition that hides the home's entrance and cloakroom from view. Sharp edges, narrow cupboards, and slender countertops give the entire room an air of lightness, while the imposing matte-black island adds depth and character to the otherwise all-white space. In addition, the considered layout is oriented towards gigantic doors and windows, which allows the owners to enjoy views of the entire space whether cooking or dining.

Sharp edges, narrow cupboards, and slender countertops give the entire room an *air of lightness*

→ *A sleek black island overlooks the garden in this minimalist kitchen, which comfortably combines a cooking and dining area in a relatively small space. White walls and a concrete floor add to the kitchen's fuss-free aesthetic.*

→ *Studio Piet Boon used Macaubas granite in different finishes to subtly separate the dining table from the cooking areas of the Edge kitchen, which features elegant details such as a sunken hob and handle-free units in gray-stained brushed oak.*

A New Way of Looking at Kitchen Living

Based in the Netherlands, Studio Piet Boon has won international acclaim for its designs, which balance "functionality, aesthetics, and individuality"—and its latest offering, created to give new meaning to the term "kitchen living," is no exception. Called the Edge, its innovative tri-point design fuses cooking, preparation, and dining areas in a single monolithic piece of furniture.

The expansive surfaces are crafted from durable Macaubas granite, while the cabinets are made from a gray-stained brushed oak. Subtle details help to define the separate functions, such as the finish on the granite: polished for the dining table and leathered for the work surfaces. "The ultimate culinary meeting point" is how Studio Piet Boon describes the Edge, which owes its name to the concept's lack of borders. "Traditional room barriers lapse and 'a place in a space' arises," explain the designers. "Various functions are seamlessly blended into one design."

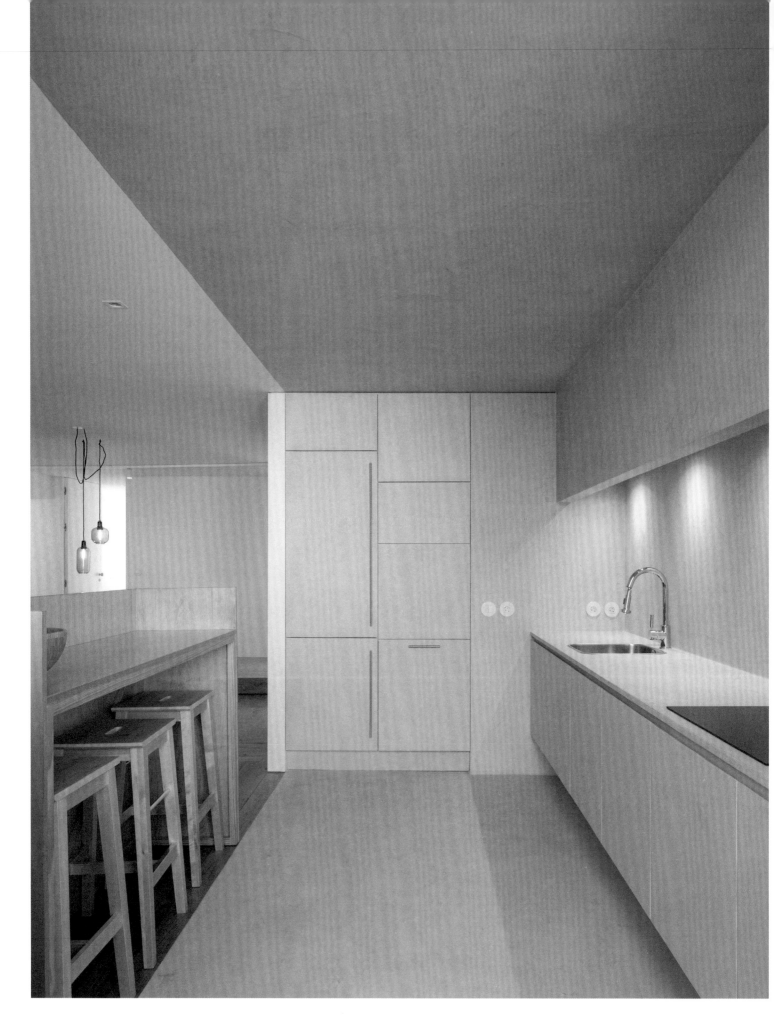

→ Beyond the brass-clad counter in the center of this open-plan space is a textural gray kitchen, which features a line of floating units and warm downlighting for subtle warmth and depth. Matching grey walls and floors create a seamless feel.

A Brilliant Brass Showpiece for a Minimalist Home

"The project was based on the idea of simplification," say Pablo Rebelo and Pedro Pita of this apartment, which is located in the Portuguese city of Porto. The pair, who founded Pablo Pita architects in 2012, applied their minimal design ethos to the once-fragmented interior of the home, reworking it with a new "night and day" layout. One side of the apartment now houses the bedrooms, while the other contains a contiguous kitchen and living area. In the middle, a curved curtain partitions the two sides while retaining an air of lightness. For the most part, the kitchen is clean lined and austere, featuring a floating bank of gray units that almost blends into the wall. At its center is a shining brass-clad counter that divides the cooking and prep areas from the living and dining space. The luminescent tones of the metal help to lessen the impact of the blocky design, at the same time adding warmth to the space, which is described by its designers as "an exercise in clarity and lightness."

→ *At the center of this light, airy space is a striking island and breakfast bar made from dark Saint Laurent marble, beyond it are tall oven units in gloss lacquer. The kitchen is part of Cesar's N_Elle collection.*

Contemporary Design with an Artisanal Past

Italian brand Cesar was founded in 1968, when Sante Vittorio Cester decided to launch his own kitchen company from his Venice workshop. One wonders whether the artisan cabinetmaker could have imagined then that his decision would eventually lead to Cesar becoming one of Italy's premier manufacturers, with a global reach and flagship stores in Milan, Paris, and New York.

"Exceptional care in the choice of materials, personalization of the product, and great attention to customer service are our fundamental values," says the brand, which aims to stay true to its origins. All of the kitchens are still made in Italy, in Pramaggiore, where Cester had his first workshop. The designs are highly customizable and available in a wide selection of finishes, from lacquers and melamine to natural woods and cement. And with a range of traditional and contemporary styles to choose from, there is something to suit every space, from stately palazzos to slick city pads.

All of the kitchens are still made in *Pramaggiore,* where Sante Vittorio Cester had his first workshop

→ *The doors of all Cesar kitchens are available in four different thicknesses, depending on the model. Each option can be fitted with a range of sleek cabinet pulls, or for a more minimal look, handles can be integrated into the design.*

Cesar

→ *Maxima 2.2 is one of the brand's most popular concepts, hailed for its versatility and practicality. The modular design has a distinctive linear quality and comes in more than 90 finishes, allowing for a high level of customization.*

Bright Ideas for a Smarter Kitchen

Cleaner air, less waste, more time, and better food... Find out how kitchen design is evolving to help improve your life

This *SmartSlab Table* was developed by Kram/Weisshaar as a testing ground for a new composite material that could allow your work surface to be used for a range of tasks, from cooking food to cooling drinks. Discreet digital devices embedded in the razor-thin ceramic top control temperature across the table.

From app-controlled ovens to "intelligent" work surfaces, there's no doubt that smart technology is changing how we use, and spend time in, our kitchens. With "connected" devices becoming ever more accessible, it's increasingly easy to integrate this kind of tech into everyday life. Whether it's entirely necessary for your fridge to remind you to buy milk is up for debate, but if the same appliance can help you streamline your shopping list and cut down on food waste, it's got to be a step in the right direction.

"For me, the big question is: 'Does it make my life easier?'" says technology journalist Chris Haslam. "A washing machine still needs loading, so using an app to turn it on and off seems a bit pointless, but I can see the benefit of using one →

You don't need an app or an expensive coffee machine to make the perfect cup of joe. Fellow's Stagg Pour-Over Kettle is foolproof. Not only does it look great, but it also includes a thermometer to ensure optimal brewing temperature and a precision spout for a slow, steady pour.

The Appliances

Falmec's Sophie extractor is one of six designs in the CircleTech collection, all of which are designed to offer superior rates of extraction thanks to an innovative filtering unit. Made of naturally occurring zeolite and activated charcoal, it was developed to both retain moisture and neutralize odors for better air quality.

The start-up Ovie has designed a food storage system to make your fridge smarter. The Smarterware line has a light ring that tells you the freshness of every tagged item in your fridge. It also connects with smart-home hubs and food apps to help you cut down on waste and do more with the food you buy.

to help choose a cycle or work out when your wash will finish." Haslam also flags troubleshooting as an underrated feature, with machines now able to warn you about blocked filters and remind you about servicing—and even order your washing powder when you've run out.

As far as an easy life goes, things are looking up for the culinarily challenged too, with a host of guided cooking apps now available. Some appliances even have this feature built in, such as the GE Kitchen Hub, which offers access to recipes and cooking guidance, as well as movies, music, and more. "It's very cool, but in truth the big touch-screen devices are simply blending two parts of our worlds: smartphones and appliances," says Haslam. "Do they need to mix? Not really, but navigating menus and settings on a well-designed app is infinitely more intuitive than using push-button controls and a tiny LCD screen."

The GE Kitchen Hub also integrates extraction into its design, which is not a particularly exciting function but one that's receiving a growing amount of attention due to the rise of open-plan living. Italian company Falmec, who take designing cooker hoods seriously, have even developed models that claim →

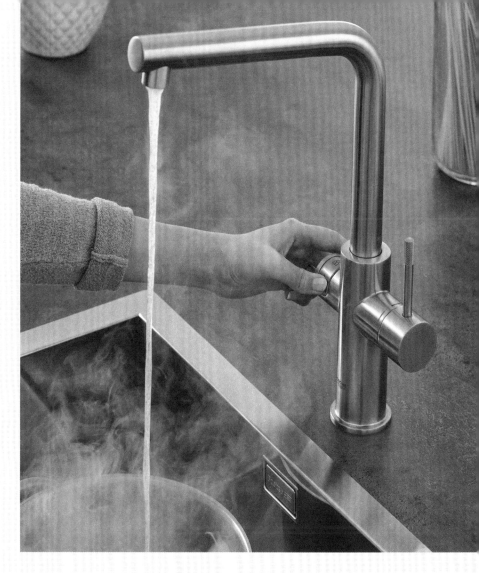

Boiling-water taps have been around for a while, but Grohe have evolved things somewhat with their Red Duo model. The design features a clever child-lock system, operated via touch buttons, which makes having a tap that instantly delivers water at 99 °C that much safer.

The Kitchen Hub by GE combines extraction with touch-screen technology. It features a camera with multiple angles so you can keep an eye on your food as it cooks, and offers access to recipes, cooking guidance, a calendar, movies, music, and more.

The 400 series of A+++ smart dishwashers by Gaggenau has zeolite technology to decrease energy consumption. An eco-friendly mineral that absorbs moisture as it releases heat, zeolite helps increase cycle speed and protects delicate glassware by drying them at a lower, gentler temperature.

Grundig's recently unveiled Connected Home collection uses projection technology to turn induction hobs into intuitive work surfaces with touch displays, through which you can control all the appliances in your kitchen, as well as mobile phones and other home tech.

to improve air quality. Is this the start of wellness-focused kitchens? Watch this space. What Haslam can predict is the continued popularity of voice control, with people already using virtual assistants as high-tech kitchen hands for tasks such as setting timers and converting weights and measures. But with devices capable of taking an increased amount of control over the cooking process, one wonders how long it will be until the roles start to reverse. Whether the prospect of Alexa cooking your dinner excites or horrifies you, it can't help but make you wonder what developments are around the corner that might previously have seemed impossible. "In a post-smartphone world, I don't think anyone thinks anything is impossible. But when we finally have OLED wallpaper and countertops that display anything we want on any surface, I think people will be suitably impressed," says Haslam. "Although I'm still waiting for the oven from *Back to the Future* that rehydrates a pizza in five seconds ..." ▬

"Oasi is a center of sharing, technology, tradition, and innovation. A real wellness oasis," says Aran Cucine of its new kitchen, created in collaboration with architect Stefano Boeri. Built around a real fruit tree, the design looks back as well as forward to promote wellbeing in the kitchen.

Kitchen: Now Loading

Prep faster, cook smarter and live better with thoughtfully designed, futuristic appliances for your kitchen

There is a growing global trend towards developing kitchen fixtures that take the guesswork out of cooking so that you can focus on what you do best. From electric cooking ranges to storage solutions that measure the freshness of produce to cut down on food waste, designers, brands, and manufacturers have crafted appliance ranges to help your kitchen run smoother and smarter via technology.

Some of these appliances keep your kitchen clean, like the modern cooker hoods from *Falmec*.

The Italian powerhouse is known for its collaborative, sustainable design approach that results in sleek designs with a twist: while each hood looks like a luxury light fixture, they exchange cooking odors for clean air by using a unique controlled ionization process. Subtle interventions like these show that when it comes to interior design, form and function can coexist.

The *Grohe* line of products also exists at the intersection of smart technology and clean forward-thinking aesthetics. Its smooth

ceramics and elegant faucets are developed with cleanliness and efficiency in mind. As such, they offer a number of touch-activated sinks and precision temperature controls to help you cook and clean in your kitchen.

For those on a quest for the perfect morning brew, American brand *Fellow* specializes in coffee equipment that pushes the boundaries of design and innovation in food technology. Born from an experiment in 2013 to find a better way to brew coffee, the Fellow line of homeware now ranges from electric kettles with refined temperature controls to pour-over filters with built-in guides to ensure every cup is perfectly proportioned.

Indeed, outfitting a smart kitchen can also mean choosing environmentally friendly appliances for a kitchen that's built to last. *Everhot* offers handcrafted cast-iron cooking ranges from its studio in England. The electric stoves and ovens are designed to distribute heat evenly without open flames or fans, which it realized was the common culprit behind dry Sunday roasts. Optimized for energy efficiency, the electric ranges operate with a minimal carbon footprint while they cook your food to perfection.

American brand *Ovie* believes that a smarter kitchen starts with food storage. The four American co-founders realized that nearly half of the food in the States went bad

before it could be eaten, so Ovie Smarterware tracks when food is opened and uses a color-coded system of lights to visually flag food that is nearing its expiration date. This data is then uploaded to a digital data cloud that can send updates on what food needs to

be eaten soon, along with recipe suggestions on how to make the most out of your groceries.

These small changes make all the difference on a larger scale: as thoughtfully designed kitchen appliances and fixtures work smarter, cleaner, faster, and with more

precision without sacrificing their visual appeal, the possibilities are endless. The future is now.

Looking for more inspiration in sourcing smart kitchen appliances? Refer to the index at the back of the book.

→ *The clean-cut stainless-steel units feature beveled doors and curved corners that help to soften the overall aesthetic.*

White Walls and Stainless Steel for Light Loft Living

Sleek, sturdy, and appropriately utilitarian, a stainless-steel Abimis kitchen was the perfect fit for this architect-designed Parisian loft. The apartment was reworked by Festen Architecture, who made the most of the high ceilings, steel structures, and wall of factory windows, which allow for spectacular views over the 10th arrondissement.

The light that fills the white-walled space is maximized by the seamless steel surfaces of Abimis's Ego model. The design has a clean-cut silhouette thanks to the beveled doors that sit flush with the surface, while curved corners help to soften the overall look of this professional-grade kitchen. In the center, a large island, fitted with an induction hob and an oven, overlooks the living room and the surrounding rooftops, while a second block beneath the window houses the sink. At the far end of the space, a simple stainless-steel-topped table links the kitchen to the dining area, resulting in a harmonious and pared-back space that allows the architecture to shine.

Joyful Minimalism in a Melbourne Apartment

This Melbourne apartment is the work of BoardGrove Architects, who reconfigured the layout to make the home lighter and more open. Part of the brief from the owners was to avoid a "stereotypical wall of kitchen joinery cupboards and appliances," which they felt would dominate the open-plan living and dining space.

"Kitchens are a good opportunity to design something special and unique. We aimed to create a slightly ambiguous cooking area that appeared as a collection of sculptural objects," say the architects, who designed the solid Corian bench, large metal arched door, and complementing arched reveal—three key elements that help to define the kitchen area. The soothing palette came about as a response to the existing apartment shell, with colors and materials chosen to complement the soft mottled tones of the concrete wall and floors. "Apartment interiors can often be predictable," they add. "This renovation attempted to achieve a more flexible and joyful living environment."

→"I love the flexibility of the design," says designer Fiona Lynch of this kitchen, which is made up of moving elements and boasts a beautiful combination of materials, including veined marble, green-tinted mirrors, and gleaming polished brass.

A Mix of Materials and Moving Parts

The kitchen of this slender Victorian terrace home in Melbourne was conceived as a series of "loose joinery objects" by design studio Fiona Lynch, allowing furniture to be moved around the space for added flexibility and interest. "Long, narrow terrace houses are always problematic as you can be constrained by the tightness of the space and lack of versatility," says Lynch. "Our approach was to design a kitchen with movable parts." As such, the fridge and pantry storage are built on castors and can be relocated when needed to free up more room for entertaining. The previous kitchen layout only allowed one person to cook at a time. "The design constrained the owners," says Lynch. "With this in mind, we actively sought to design a space with a sense of freedom." Not just practical, the new kitchen is elegant too, composed of a rich mix of materials, from green French mirrors to veined marble and polished brass. Oak cabinetry painted in a soft, plaster-like tone completes the sophisticated aesthetic.

Design for Healthy Habits and Sustainable Living

You might be surprised to the learn that part of the kitchen of this 1950s villa, located to the north of Copenhagen and home to kitchen designer Helle Jensen, is made from an unusual material: corn. Created by German brand Rotpunkt—which is stocked by Jensen's company, Haus and Honey—the kitchen is made from bio-board, a more eco-friendly chipboard consisting of non-edible corn and 37 percent less wood than ususal. Complementing this is a wall of specially treated sustainable cork—an affordable and textural backdrop to the white-and-wood design, which features a second unit made from warm oak. This sociable, family-friendly kitchen was designed with healthy eating in mind, so the central island unit features a spacious countertop and sink rather than a hob—ideal for those who spend more time preparing simple meals made from fresh vegetables than cooking complex dishes. A boiling-water tap was fitted to make blanching produce quick and easy, while a sparkling-water tap keeps kids' soda consumption to a minimum.

→ *Functional wall panels are an optional part of all Henrybuilt kitchens. They allow an additional level of integration with the architecture, while making the whole space more functional. Wooden or steel shelves can also be integrated into the backsplash system.*

Expertly Crafted Solutions for the Smart Kitchen

American company Henrybuilt was founded in 2001 in a shed on Vashon Island in Washington State. Since then, the brand has completed more than 4,000 projects and has multiple showrooms across the U.S. Its work blends traditional craftsmanship with high-quality integrated design to create hardworking personalized kitchens and storage.

Take the design of its Fluted Island: pulling any one of its darkened brass handles reveals a "network of smart storage." Its nine drawers, which can be fitted with various wooden dividers to further compartmentalize the contents, offer a perfectly organized home for everything from condiments to pots and pans. "Our systems combine handcrafted beauty with years of focused product design and refinement, resulting in an industrially engineered product that is also adaptable to your space," says the brand of its range, which also includes the popular Functional Partition Wall. One side of the wall serves as a semi-transparent room divider, while the other provides valuable and easily accessible storage.

"Handcrafted *beauty* meets years of focused *product design* and refinement"

→ *One side of this Functional Partition Wall serves as a semi-transparent room divider, while the other provides valuable and easily accessible storage.*

→ *The Fluted Island features a "network of smart storage" configured across nine drawers, which can be fitted with various wooden dividers to further compartmentalize the contents, offering a perfectly organized home for everything from condiments to pots and pans.*

→ *Brass accents and a polished pine floor warm up this Baltimore kitchen, which strikes a balance of dark and light. The white wall-hung cabinets and Carrara marble backsplash help to lessen the impact of the dark-painted cabinetry below.*

Modern Meets Traditional in This Monochrome Space

Dark cabinetry and a nod to Nordic style were the main requirements for the new kitchen of this home in Baltimore, U.S. The owners enlisted Maryland-based interior designer Elizabeth Lawson for the project, who set about meeting the brief while trying to create a space that felt light and airy at the same time. To achieve this, she combined dark-painted lower units with white wall-hung cabinets and a continuous backsplash in white Carrara marble. Open shelving also features and is used for displaying neat stacks of white plates and glassware so as not to compromise the space's streamlined feel.

"Aesthetically, we aimed to marry both traditional and modern elements," says Lawson, who fitted Shaker-style cabinets made from solid maple with slender brass handles, and opted for a classic apron sink. Other metallic touches—such as the faucet, wall lights, and island pendants—add a subtle touch of luxe, while a patterned runner builds on the warmth and character of the heart-pine floor.

Elizabeth Lawson Design

Bespoke Design with an Architectural Lean

German brand Holzrausch was founded by friends and master carpenters Sven Petzold and Tobias Petri in 1998. Since then, the studio has grown into a talented assembly of architects, interior designers, wood technicians, and joiners. Kitchens are at the core of their work, which involves planning, designing, and building architecturally and spatially sensitive furniture. Honing a timeless, minimalist design language has been essential to the brand's success. "We place great value on the emotional effect of material and every single detail," say Petzold and Petri. "Every piece is one of a kind."

Holzrausch produces all of its kitchens and interior fittings in its own workshops. "We are able to truly practice a craft and to work with our hands," add the founders. Wood, glass, steel, natural stone, and cement play a role in most projects, with much time and care spent selecting the right materials. "Quality and craftsmanship will never be just a fleeting trend; you notice when furniture has been made with love."

→ *The master carpenters at Holzrausch are renowned for clever, well-crafted solutions, such as the hidden appliances and storage in this wall of built-in cabinetry. Smart details, like the perfectly proportioned coffee station, help keep surfaces free of clutter.*

→ *This project saw a vast hall transformed into a kitchen-living space, with a striking counter at its center, which is made from granite and a burnished brass alloy called tombak. The fronts and fittings are crafted from stained ash.*

→ *Holzrausch teamed up Munich-based product and design studio OHA for this project, who created the door handles from scratch. "It is the perfect example of an industrial kitchen system created with a craftsman's mind," say Holzrausch.*

A Minimalist Take on Luxe Materials

Award-wining design studio Fiona Lynch is behind the renovation of this 150-year-old Victorian terrace in Sydney's Surry Hills. The first task was to rearrange all interior spaces to make the most of the narrow floor plan, before introducing a scheme the studio describes as "light and luxurious." The only exception to the airy aesthetic is the navy kitchen, designed to be the pièce de résistance of the home, which is owned by two keen cooks who love to entertain. "An inventive use of space, materials, and custom detailing are the creative hallmarks of our practice," says Lynch. "As is a tailored and meticulous approach to understanding the needs of our clients." The deep-blue American oak joinery features a high-gloss finish, lessening the impact of the dark color choice, while a mix of Carrara marble, Elba stone, terrazzo, and polished brass help to lighten the look. The overall effect is characteristically Lynch, harnessing, as she puts it, "the quiet brilliance of minimalism and materiality with lasting impact."

Step Inside an Adaptable *Backyard* Kitchen in Berkeley

Californian photographer Erin Scott turned a garden cottage into a multi–purpose studio space that doubles as a kitchen

Erin Scott

Part shoot kitchen, part photography studio, this 46 m² (500 ft²) space is located in the backyard of Berkeley-based photographer Erin Scott. The Californian cottage was formerly a garage, office, and tool shed, until she brought in friend and architect Abigail Turin of Kallos Turin to overhaul it. "As my food photography career took off, I dreamed of converting our cottage into a photography studio with a full kitchen," says Scott. "After years of wishing, I partnered up with Abigail to get serious about designing it."

"I knew I wanted an airy, white, flexible space which could be used in a myriad of ways depending on the needs of each photography project," she adds, "so we opened up the room completely, added a kitchen, office area, and shoot space, plus ample shelving." Aided by local builder Matt Hooven, Scott and Turin designed an efficient kitchen that runs along one wall, complete with a Lacanche range cooker and white stone surfaces that mimic marble, but come at a fraction of the cost. "Even though I wanted the flexibility of a simple white space, I also wanted a few luxurious touches," says Scott. "The beautiful enamel Lacanche stove was the first thing I bought—we basically designed the kitchen around it."

The finished interior has a practical and inexpensive concrete floor, and a "soft, chalky, and tonal" scheme that is the perfect backdrop for Scott's vast collection of styling props and ceramics. "Everything in the kitchen has a double function: each tool, bowl, cutting board, or knife is practical enough to cook with and beautiful enough to photograph," she explains. Open shelving was chosen to keep costs down, as well as to allow items to be accessed quickly and easily on shoots. "I've had to use all sorts of containers in a creative way," adds Scott. "Little vintage bread tins are used to store knives,

→ Scott opted for a hardwearing stone for the countertop and backsplash that looks similar to marble, but is much more affordable.

sponges, and clothes pins. Baskets of all shapes and sizes hold bigger items like linens, baking sheets, and camera gear, while ceramic jars make perfect pots for cutlery and utensils."

Due to the dual-purpose nature of the space, flexibility is key, so many features are adaptable—from the curtains, which are hung from brass clips, to a rolling workbench and shelving unit. Even the raw elm desktop in Scott's office area doubles as extra kitchen and shoot space when required. Lighting is highly customizable too, with power outlets set into the exposed ceiling beams to allow the hanging bulbs to be moved around as needed, and with blackout blinds fitted to windows to control natural light coming in from outside. The overall result is an open and inviting space that is a pleasure to spend time in, whether working or otherwise. "You really feel like you're out in the garden even though you're inside," says its contented owner. "On non-shoot days, I'm usually hosting a lunch or tea. A few people have walked in and said it feels like a potter's studio—I love that. I wanted to create somewhere my collaborators and I feel inspired to work, craft, and create." ▪

"As my food photography career took off, I dreamed of converting our cottage into a photography studio and kitchen"

→ *Flexibility is the key to this space. Many features are adaptable, such as the rolling workbench and shelving unit. Even the raw elm desktop in Scott's office area doubles as extra kitchen and shoot space when required.*

→ *Power outlets in the ceiling beams allow the hanging bulbs to be moved around as needed, and the curtains are hung from brass clips, making the lighting highly customizable. Blackout blinds can be fitted to the windows when shooting too.*

Design with Urban Life in Mind

This apartment, situated in Vienna's 8th district, was recently updated by Kombinat Arhitekti to make it better suited to the dynamic nature of contemporary city living. Set in an early twentieth-century building with high ceilings and spacious rooms, the renovation restored the original layout, with a living area facing the busy street and bedrooms looking out onto a quiet courtyard.

Partition walls were removed to create a large room that contains the new kitchen-diner, the core element of which is a wall of cabinets that encompasses both the cooking area and a window seat overlooking the street. "First and foremost, this is a place to gather and meet," say Kombinat Arhitekti, who used solid ash for the cabinetry and the tall freestanding shelving unit, which weaves the fridge and oven into its design. At the far end of the kitchen, two comfy armchairs offer a spot to relax and spend time with whoever's turn it is to cook, while the long table can double as a workspace when required.

Two comfy armchairs offer *a spot to relax* and spend time with whoever's turn it is to cook

→ *The kitchen of this Viennese apartment provides numerous different spots to work, lounge or dine, from the raised window seat (complete with backrest), which doubles as a desk, to the cosy armchairs and the extra-long dining table.*

An Unexpected Take on Understated Luxury

A striking color scheme defines this kitchen in a family home in Charlottenburg, Berlin, designed by interiors and architecture firm Gisbert Pöppler. The studio rearranged the property's existing layout and installed a custom-made kitchen conceived to satisfy the requirements of modern day family life. "We combined the functionality needed for the busiest part of the home with a beautiful environment to live in," says Gisbert Pöppler, who introduced an "element of understated luxury" through the chosen colors, placing bold turquoise alongside deep green and soft salmon pink. A dark Silestone countertop adds punch, as does the black wire glass backsplash, while brass accents continue the air of refinement suggested by the home's original parquet flooring. The designers cite a comprehensive understanding of space, color, and light as being integral to the studio's work, which sees "exuberant flourishes tempered with Northern European restraint creating harmonious hybrids of unexpected elegance."

→ *Bold turquoise, deep green, and salmon pink define this kitchen designed by Gisbert Pöppler, who introduced an "element of understated luxury" through the chosen color palette.*

"We combined the *functionality* needed for the busiest part of the home with a beautiful environment to live in"

→ *The Berlin-based studio cites a comprehensive understanding of space, color, and light as being integral to all projects.*

Workstead

A Finely Crafted Fusion of Past and Present

Located in Charleston, South Carolina, this former carriage house has been given a new lease of life by father-and-son team Jim and Chris Sloggatt, who meticulously renovated the outbuilding and turned it into a two-story home. They enlisted Brooklyn and Charleston-based studio Workstead to design the interiors, whose impressive portfolio of projects celebrates "utility, form, and material strength."

"The new kitchen serves as the literal and figurative heart of the home," says the studio, referencing the grand central island with its Lacanche range cooker, "around which life revolves." Built-in cupboards tucked under the stairs provide ample storage, painted black to contrast with the plaster-speckled brick walls. In the dining area, cane-fronted cypress cabinets made by artisan woodworker Clay Richardson add an air of refinement; nestled between them is a cozy windowseat that overlooks the garden. "At the heart of the carriage house is connection," say its designers, "with time and place, as well as with collaborators."

The Art of Setting the Table

Turn a humble kitchen supper into a stylish soirée with luxurious linens, statement tableware, and a few insider tips

The Table

Australia's Atelier Studios sells Mediterranean-inspired tableware that's handmade in Southern Italy by skilled ceramicists. "By choosing these products, we celebrate both their visual beauty and imperfection, as well as their longevity, functionality, and techniques rooted in tradition," says the studio.

Ever wondered how some people just seem to have a knack for entertaining, no matter how small the apartment or how simple the food? Copenhagen-based photographer and stylist Signe Bay, whose effortlessly beautiful dining scenes have garnered her a global following, says it's all about a warm welcome. "I always set the table before guests arrive, but in an informal way. I want everyone to feel relaxed and to make themselves at home."

One look at Bay's Instagram account will have you longing for a dinner invitation, revealing images of rustic tabletops, rumpled linens, and loosely arranged displays of wildflowers and foliage. "I usually finish cooking after everyone has arrived, while chatting and enjoying a glass of wine. I think it keeps →

If Scandinavian minimalism is your thing, look no further than Danish brand Normann Copenhagen for expertly designed, aesthetically pleasing kitchen equipment that's far too stylish to keep in the cupboard. Its mostly monochrome collection is interspersed with pieces in warm wood, marble, and bronze.

Laura Görs is a Berlin-based designer with "curiosity for food, cooking, and tableware." Her Salé collection, created specifically for serving fine seafood and caviar, is crafted from a mixture of glass and porcelain, and finished with different techniques to create subtly contrasting textures.

Nothing rounds off a meal like a beautifully presented cheese platter—also the perfect accompaniment for relaxed drinks. With its clean lines and leather handle, DOIY's acacia-wood cheeseboard is ideal. It even comes with two magnetized knives, the designs inspired by Swiss cheese.

the mood casual," she continues. The quiet elegance of her hosting style is, in part, down to a less-is-more approach, preferring what she describes as a "clean base" that allows both food and flowers to shine. Raw and natural textures keep table settings feeling warm and laidback, and are the perfect canvas for modern or vintage crockery. "I love contemporary ceramics, but some of my favorite pieces were found in flea markets or in antique shops. And I've inherited several candle holders and vases from my family," says Bay, who also recommends secondhand for anyone shopping on a limited budget. "Try hunting for cutlery, old ceramic plates, and cups in thrift stores. I've found lots of old tablecloths too, some handmade with the most beautiful embroidery."

The trick to combining old and new, she advises, is to keep to the same palette in terms of both color and texture—just one example of a small detail that can make all the difference. "I always try to adjust the color of the flowers to the rest of the setting too. For example, if the tablecloth and napkins are in beige linen, and the ceramics are in soft colors, the floral display should be natural and earthy," she says. As for formal dining, →

Proving that even the simplest sustenance takes on new meaning when savored properly, Laura Görs's Sensorium tray is intended for serving bread and butter. The tray's design invites you to eat with your hands and is divided into unglazed and glazed parts for dry and moist foods.

These salt and pepper shakers, by Japanese designer Nendo, aim to turn an everyday act into a playful ritual. The seasoning, contained in the small glass bottle, is poured onto the glass holder and then ground with the base of the bottle, ready to be sprinkled on food.

157

A beloved British brand established in the late 1960s by a silversmith turned Royal Designer for Industry, David Mellor Design has an international reputation for timeless, finely crafted cutlery. That said, don't overlook its equally enduring craft pottery and high-quality woodware.

Danish brand Hay has a knack for elevating everyday objects—the Rhom Trivet being a perfect example. With its distinctive rhombus shape and sturdy heat-resistant silicone, it not only looks good, but will also protect your table from hot pans and dishes, making serving that much simpler.

Bay believes a few tweaks are all that's needed to subtly elevate the occasion. "I would iron the tablecloth, but I'd still choose linen because of its amazing texture. And I'd opt for a more sculptural floral display." Statement glassware is another quick fix for smartening up your supper—a versatile investment that can be easily dressed up or down to fit the mood. "I love old vintage crystal glasses; the champagne ones have a splendid shape. They look great paired with ceramic beakers for a more relaxed setting, or with matching water glasses for added grandeur."

Whatever the occasion, Bay believes a restrained palette is the secret to stylish dining, allowing the food to take center stage. She recommends colorful salads and veg-filled dishes topped with fresh herbs, nuts, and seeds for a feast that looks as good as it tastes. But above all, ambience is key. "It's about the atmosphere you create," she concludes. "Put on some good jazz, light the candles, and get cozy."

As well as an array of French country antiques, Paris-based Madame de la Maison sells its own line of table linen, which is ethically produced and made from biodegradable fibers. Manufactured locally, the linens are available in a range of shades, and can be elegantly monogrammed if required.

A Seat at the Table

A beautifully laid table can elevate the simplest of settings. Discover everything you need to impress your guests

While the food should steal the scene at any dinner party, table settings are an opportunity to set the stage. As a host, you can choose between brass cutlery, hand-glazed plates, modern glassware, and embroidered napkins. These subtle choices can spell out the difference between a casual but refined supper club and a lavish affair.

It starts with the textiles. Soft-as-butter cotton or rough-cut linen? Solid or patterned? Matching placemats and table runners, or simple but tasteful napkins? Brands such as Italy's *Society Limonta* and Denmark's *Broste Copenhagen* offer a wide palette of choices, while *Normann Copenhagen* stocks linens alongside full furniture sets to help you find the perfect fit. Not that it's necessary: sturdy, stylish, and portable, quality textiles are easy to swap in and out as you search for the perfect harmony between homewares.

Table linens exist in conversation with serving dishes and utensils, so striking a balance of materials, textures, and colors is key to setting the mood. If you're searching for rustic, grounded charm, *Andrea Brugi* in Italy offers striking wooden boards, spoons, and stools.

The craftsman grew up in the Tuscan countryside, and the simplicity of a life lived among olive trees is infused in each of his pieces. Finding beauty in natural imperfections also comes easily to Skye Corewijn, the founder of east London pottery studio *Lazy Eye Ceramics*, whose rough-textured handcrafted tableware is favored by local Michelin-starred chefs like James Lowe. For a more polished table setting, one might look to the delicate porcelain homewares by *Rosenthal*. A heritage brand founded in the nineteenth century, the expertly designed ceramics have stood the test of time and the manufacturer continues to champion quality and sophistication to this day. Whether sleek and thoughtful or homely and warm, dinnerware presents ample ground to balance the tone of a meal from start to finish.

In many families, cutlery is a treasured heirloom for its durable elegance and practical utility, as well as for the stories passed down from generation to generation. *Madame de la Maison* in Paris took this to heart. After an initial consultation with hosts about the events they are planning, the Madame de la Maison team assembles a collection of antique tablewares. With well-loved cutlery and linens for hire or purchase, the maison brings the storied charm of heirlooms wherever they may be needed.

For those looking to forge new traditions, handcrafted stemware and crystal glasses might be the answer.

Quality wine glasses and carafes are often both stylish and resistant to scratches and cracks, like those from Austrian design house *Zalto*, which focuses on mouth-blown stemware for fine wines. Italian manufacturer *Ichendorf* offers glassware that's meant to be enjoyed as well. Its collections span the decades since it was founded in a small town outside of Cologne, and the timeless silhouettes are a distinguished guest for dinners now and in the years to come. For plates and bowls, finding the right set comes down to finding the glazes and finishes for what you're serving. A matte slate might work best with honey-glazed carrots, but a glossy finish would bring out the vibrance of fresh leaves and salads.

Setting the table is about bringing balance and harmony to the dining room, and at the end of the day, finding the perfect dinnerware is like the guest list itself—an art form, not a science.

Need inspiration for what to buy for the perfect dinner? Refer to the index at the back of the book.

→ A homely, rustic feel unites Lokal's six apartments, which have farmhouse-style tables, spindle-back chairs and sections of weathered wooden panelling. Jersey Ice Cream Co. opted for accents of blue throughout to keep the spaces cohesive.

A Hotel Kitchen
That Feels like Home

This nineteenth century building in Philadelphia is design studio Jersey Ice Cream Co's first hotel project. Tara Mangini and Percy Bright were brought in to design Lokal's six apartments for short- and long-term guests. "We wanted to create a space that felt more like home than a hotel and could accommodate living like a local," says the duo. "That meant having everything from basic essentials to crockery you could proudly set a table with, as well as proper cooking utensils. The things we take for granted at home really make a difference when you're on the road."

The units feature capacious kitchens with everything one needs to cook and eat comfortably, including full-height fridges, induction hobs, speed convection ovens, and roomy dining tables. With its modern farmhouse aesthetic, the design is distinctly Jersey Ice Cream Co. Bold blue-green cabinetry (painted in Sherwin-Williams's Seaworthy shade) sings when paired with brass tapware and handles, while open shelves display crockery, glassware, and artwork for a home-away-from-home feel.

"The things we take for granted at home really *make a difference* when you're on the road"

→ *Seaworthy paint by Sherwin-Williams has been used on the window frames, skirting boards, and kitchen cabinetry, adding character without overpowering the space. Aged leather, textural rugs, brass details and a mix of woods create a lived-in feel.*

→ *Mayan-inspired architecture meets low-key luxury in this refreshingly simple and earthy space, crafted solely from concrete and timber. The only conspicuously contemporary additions are the stainless-steel appliances that have been integrated into the design.*

Organic and Natural in a Historic Hacienda

Located on the Yucatán Peninsula, less than an hour from the city of Mérida, Hacienda Tamchen is part of a breathtakingly beautiful seventeenth-century estate. The property had been abandoned for more than 80 years by 2009, when it was painstakingly restored by Muñoz Arquitectos. The sensitive renovation of the four-bedroom property marries Mayan-inspired architecture with an air of low-key luxury, resulting in a boxy structure with a rugged interior of ancient stone and cool concrete.

Modern elements have been introduced carefully, which is why the kitchen has been designed with such refreshing simplicity. Organic yet minimal, the concrete forms are barely distinguishable from the surrounding interior architecture, while rough-hewn timber doors serve as cabinet fronts. Open shelving displays an array of earthy ceramics, again, hardly noticeable against the rough stone walls; the only obviously contemporary additions are the stainless-steel appliances that have been integrated into the design.

Resourceful Solutions and Reclaimed Finds

Fashion designer Anna-Tina Schaal and her husband, Andreas, a business consultant, are the creative brains behind the design of this monochrome kitchen, which they dreamt up for their Cape Town home. A palette of black, white, and stainless steel presides in the space, which is screened by custom metal frames that double as a safety rail for the stairs leading to the floor below. Many of the pieces tell a story, such as the 1950s Frigidaire, which was gifted by friends and family, and has been painted black to match the cabinets and wall of glossy metro tiles. In the center of the kitchen, an island unit divides the cooking space from the dining area, clad on one side with reclaimed wood that was salvaged from the property during its renovation. Above the island is a light fitting of the couple's own design: a simple powder-coated bar hung with cable cords and vintage-style bulbs. Even the tap was a bespoke job, configured using various elements from the hardware store and a piece of brass pipe bent into a spout.

Anna-Tina & Andreas Schaal

→ *A palette of black, white, and stainless steel presides in this Cape Town kitchen, which belongs to fashion designer Anna-Tina Schaal and her husband, Andreas. A 1950s Frigidaire has been painted black to match the cabinets and glossy metro tiles.*

Many of the pieces tell a story, such as the *1950s Frigidaire*, which was gifted by friends and family

→ *In the center of the kitchen, an island unit—clad on one side with reclaimed wood that was salvaged from the property during its renovation—divides the cooking space from the dining area. Above this is a light fitting of the couple's own design.*

A Vibrant Update for a Retro Residence

This 1970s town house in Melbourne's Fitzroy North suburb is home to architect-owner Lisa Breeze, who has been steadily renovating the property over a number of years. One of the main achievements to date is the inviting kitchen, which is resplendent in a steely shade of blue and was reworked with a more efficient, less space-hungry layout. "Cues from salvaged building elements, such as timber wall paneling and painted bricks, influence the new features," says Breeze, who introduced refined finishes and strong colors alongside the "humble elements" of the original architecture, celebrating the home's subtle retro feel. The factory-painted joinery features routed line work in a custom pattern to mimic a paneled effect, while countertops are made from Super White Quartzite—a hardier option than marble. "The new features are basic," she adds, "with textured forms standing strong against the classic brickwork and rough sawn timber joists above." Outside, a tiny garden acts as an extension of the kitchen when the weather permits.

Lisa Breeze

Handmade Kitchens with a Heritage of Design

British brand deVOL has been producing handmade kitchens in Leicester since 1989. Its finely crafted designs strike a balance between tradition and modernity, as illustrated by the vibrant teal Shaker-style kitchen the brand created for an Edwardian home in London. Cabinetry was designed to conceal as many appliances as possible to help the kitchen look like an extension of the living space. "This makes it feel more like the center of the action rather than an afterthought or a place for doing chores," say the designers.

Different in style but equally striking is the Sebastian Cox kitchen, named after the east London studio deVOL collaborated with. Here, the focus is on the raw beauty of the sustainable British-grown timbers used, on the birch plywood carcasses and beech cabinet doors. In the kitchen of this Bath home, a blend of dark and natural finishes were paired with concrete floors and countertops, copper, and expanses of glass for a look that is part industrial, part artisanal.

→ deVOL's Classic English Kitchen range is inspired by period Georgian and farmhouse kitchens. Totally bespoke, these kitchens can be made in any size and with any finish. The brand's mission is to "continue a tradition of English carpentry made to the highest quality."

Hiding away appliances gives a room a *furnished feel* that's more akin to a living space

→ *This teal Shaker-style kitchen was built for an Edwardian home in London; the cabinetry was designed to conceal as many appliances as possible.*

→ deVOL collaborated with London design studio Sebastian Cox for this kitchen, which focuses on the raw beauty of wood and uses sustainably grown British timber such as birch plywood and beech.

→ *The Sebastian Cox kitchen in this home in Bath pairs a blend of dark and natural finishes with concrete floors and countertops, copper, and expanses of glass for a look that is part industrial, part artisanal.*

History Revisited in a Berlin Apartment

When German stylist Thomas Rook first looked round the 1901 tenement apartment in Berlin that he would come to call home, he was overjoyed to discover that all of its period features had been perfectly preserved. He embarked on a sensitive restoration that updated the flat for modern living but retained its original soul. "I changed the entire floor plan in order to have more space for cooking and entertaining guests," says Rook, who built his new kitchen where there was once a bedroom. An unexpected mix of styles, the finished space pairs understated black cabinets with dusky pink tiles from Berlin brand Golem, which specializes in the reproduction of architectural ceramics and art nouveau tiles.

Verde Marinace granite was used for the work surfaces, which complement the blue-green tones of the walls. "I wanted to mix colors that are cheerful but not too bright," Rook explains. The quirky and traditional come together for an air of overt homeliness—from the Bavarian cuckoo clock to the 1920s fringed ceiling pendant.

"I changed the entire floor plan in order to have *more space* for cooking and entertaining guests"

→ *The quirky and traditional come together for an air of overt homeliness in Thomas Rook's apartment—from the Bavarian cuckoo clock and fringed ceiling pendant to the antique cabinet that's used to display a mix of ornate glassware and vintage finds.*

A Quirky Home with a Dark Side

This unusual home is located in
a former Royal Navy Air Squadron
control tower on Easter Airfield,
some 35 kilometers (22 miles) north of
Inverness in the Scottish Highlands.
During the Second World War, it
was used as a base for torpedo-carrying
aircraft; today, it belongs to Justin
Hooper and Charlotte Seddon, who
dedicated much time and effort to
the restoration of the tower, named
HMS Owl. For the new kitchen,
the pair turned to British Standard
(sister company to Plain English),
who worked with the couple to devise a
design that would feel at home inside
the hard-edged building. Due to HMS
Owl's abundance of large Crittall
windows, the interior is flooded with
light throughout the day, which
meant Hooper and Seddon could opt
for a dramatic dark scheme. Black
paint was applied to cupboard doors
and part of the walls, the top section
of which has been left unpainted
to avoid cramping the space. Iroko
hardwood was chosen for the countertops, while an Aga forms a homely
centerpiece and pours out heat during
the long, cold winters.

We were keen to design a kitchen that felt *at home* in the wartime control tower

→ *British Standard worked closely with Hooper and Seddon to create a concept that would feel in keeping with the architecture but suitable for a residential project. Exposed brick and plasterwork combine with black-painted units to dramatic effect.*

HMS Owl's kitchen is *dark and dramatic,* with hardwood countertops and dark–painted cupboards

→ An Aga fills one end of the kitchen, blending in with the black-painted units on either side of the horseshoe-shaped layout. The dark paint extends to backsplash height, above this, the wall has been left unpainted for a roomier feel.

Sixties Style Brought Back to Life with a Sustainable Twist

Salvaged materials meet an eclectic mix of influences in this Australian eco-home

Etica Studio

→ Sustainability focused Etica Studio designed this eco-house to be a nature-inspired hideaway for its owner, the architect's sister. The solar-passive home runs on renewable energy and was built using a mix of environmentally friendly materials and salvaged elements.

Tucked away on a narrow lane in Perth, Western Australia, this compact eco-house has been imagined as a nature-inspired hideaway by sustainable design firm Etica Studio, founded by architect Carla Karsakis. The solar-passive home runs on renewable energy and was built using a mix of eco-friendly materials and salvaged elements, such as its double-height wall made from reclaimed windows. The external structure is made from rammed earth and concrete rubble (that would otherwise have gone to landfill), with other recycled elements used throughout—from 1960s bricks to 100-year-old pine floorboards.

The design was conceived in collaboration with the architect's sister Tanya McKenna and her partner, Peter Chadwick, who own the home. They drew from a "rich palette of eclectic references" for the interiors, ranging from a love of Scandinavia and South America to an appreciation of mid-century design and a preference for "honest materiality." For the kitchen, the goal was to create a light, bright, café-style entertaining space. Brazilian architecture informed the concrete backdrop, while a penchant for 1960s design inspired the pale timber-and-ply units and the graphic, grid-like tiled countertops. Fremantle-based furniture makers Raw Edge crafted the cabinetry; other timber pieces, such as the box light suspended above the island, were made by Chadwick. "We wanted to integrate more sustainable elements and reclaimed materials," says Karsakis, "so we sourced the Oregon bench top from an old pub outside Perth." Other requirements on the wish list included a large work surface, areas for display, and separate zones for cooking, preparation, serving, and entertaining. One of the major challenges the architect faced

→ *The Oregon wood used for the countertop on the island unit is reclaimed, and came from an old pub on the outskirts of Perth.*

was designing the kitchen beneath the staircase. "I needed to make sure this wouldn't impact on the overall look," she explains. "And from a detail perspective, designing exact dimensions around the two different sizes of tiles was very challenging as we wanted to avoid cutting them." A lot of time and thought went into ensuring that the combination of materials worked. "I love how the different uses of materials delineate separate spaces and functions, such as the tiled areas for preparation and cooking and the Oregon wood for serving and entertaining," she adds. The finished space is relaxed and airy, with the casual, café-style feel that the trio set out to achieve. Favorite details include the hit of forest green introduced with the painted pantry cupboard and the home's front door—McKenna tried six different shades before finding the perfect hue—and the tiled plinth behind the stove area. The latter acts as additional storage to keep the countertop free of clutter, as well as serving as a display space that gives the kitchen its personal feel. The ply and Oregon elements offset the rawness of the concrete walls, while the pale polished floor and white tiles bounce the abundant light around the space. ▪

"I love how the different uses of materials delineate the separate spaces and functions"

→ *A pale polished floor helps to bounce around the light that floods in through the double-height wall of reclaimed windows. Accents of green and wooden pieces add to the nature-inspired feel.*

A Playful Contrast of Old and New

Located in the Barcelona neighborhood of Gràcia, this rectangular flat was reworked by interiors and architecture firm Cirera + Espinet, who removed all partition walls and implemented built-in and modular furniture solutions to define the space instead. Subtle nods to industrial style can be seen throughout, particularly in the kitchen, where a stainless-steel island provides the main cooking space, complete with an overhead gantry that contains an exposed extraction unit. A tiled dining table on castors (the studio's own design) extends into an adjacent area clad entirely in pale fir wood, while mint-green melamine furniture interacts playfully with the well-worn ceiling beams. "This project is an exercise in what we love doing best," say the designers, who favor contrasting materials, like the stainless steel that juxtaposes beautifully with the timber floor, ceiling, and walls. "Our style prioritizes function, but with harmonious and eclectic elements that give personality and character to a space."

An All-Green Backdrop for Added Impact

When design agency Atelier Sagitta overhauled this Parisian apartment to make more room to accommodate its owners' two young children, the stylish new kitchen was an added bonus. The studio used an arresting green floor-to-ceiling scheme to define the cooking and dining areas, which are located within the downstairs open-plan living space of this two-story apartment. They then installed a bespoke handcrafted kitchen with copious amounts of storage, including a large stand-alone cabinet with sliding doors to conceal all the necessary cooking appliances.

All frames, supports, and work surfaces were crafted from solid oak sourced within Île-de-France, while casements and fronts were built using a more affordable birch plywood. A matte white finish, combined with the warm timber details, was chosen as a fresh and timeless contrast to the deep-green backdrop, while slatted cupboard fronts and lower units raised on feet stop the design from feeling too heavy in the small space.

A *green scheme* defines the cooking and dining areas, which are located within the open–plan living space

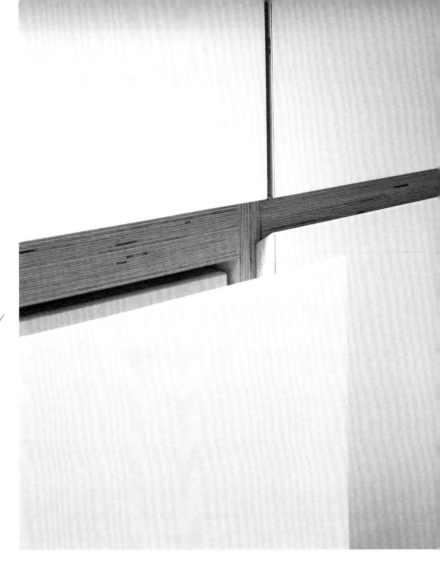

→ *Design agency Atelier Sagitta chose the striking green floor-to-ceiling backdrop to help define the cooking and dining areas, which are located within the downstairs open-plan living space of this two-story apartment.*

A Design That Evolves with the Times

Aware of the expense of keeping up with changing trends, the founders of Copenhagen store Stilleben, Ditte Reckweg and Jelena Schou, decided it was time someone created an updatable kitchen. So the duo joined forces with architect Trine Hjorth and cabinetmaker Ditlev Rahbek of HjorthRahbek Arkitekter to devise a range of practical kitchens than can be repainted as tastes evolve.

"We wanted to make a kitchen that can handle changing times," say Reckweg and Schou. "Something that's classic in design but contemporary in color and fitted with modern solutions." The kitchens are made up of a basic core design with hand-painted cabinets, so that if you go off the color and wish to freshen it up, you can easily do so.

"Everything should be made to last for a very long time—longer than normal," say Stilleben Kitchen's founders. As such, drawers are made of solid oak with durable dovetail joints. Other than this, everything is customizable, including countertops, appliances, colors, and hardware.

→ *Stilleben's kitchen series can be repainted to move with the times. Opt for a neutral shade or be brave and try out a stronger color. If you change your mind, updating the cabinetry couldn't be simpler.*

→ *The kitchen is a basic core design with drawers made of solid oak and durable dovetail joints. Other than this, everything is customizable, including countertops, appliances, colors, and hardware.*

"We wanted to make a kitchen that's classic in design but *contemporary* in color and fitted with modern solutions"

→ *Sydney studio Minosa Design used lime-washed oak, Dekton Sirocco gray countertops, and handmade warm white butcher tiles to keep this kitchen feeling light and open. A hint of pink helps to lift the scheme, while black accents add definition.*

Substance, Style, and Cleverly Configured Storage

Located in Paddington, Sydney, this reconstructed terrace home is the work of Minosa Design, which was enlisted by the client for the third time to create "the best kitchen yet." A statement scheme was a must, as was space for entertaining and lots of storage for appliances. "Expectations were high," say the designers. "With two successfully completed kitchens, we knew the level of quality they desired."

Minosa opted for a U-shaped layout with central island and a separate run of joinery to allow the sink plumbing to be relocated easily. This created space for the long list of appliances, which included two dishwashers, a separate steam oven, and a large integrated fridge. Finishes were chosen to keep the space feeling refined, light, and open: lime-washed oak, Dekton Sirocco gray countertops, and handmade warm white butcher tiles. The latter even cover the large door leading to the garage. A hint of pink was introduced to lift the scheme and create a focal point, while black accents add definition.

Small and Mighty *Solutions*

Transform a tiny kitchen with compact appliances, multitasking furniture, smart storage, and a seamless feel

This portable design for millennials is the brainchild of Yu Li, a graduate of London's Royal College of Art. The lightweight seven-in-one set comprises a chopping board, an induction hob, a pot and pan, a wrap for utensils and cutlery, and a drying rack in one tiny box.

When designing a small kitchen, planning is everything—but first, it's a good idea to do a ruthless assessment of your possessions to make sure you're not hanging onto superfluous equipment. Once you know how much storage you need, you can start planning the layout. If you love to cook, you'll need to think of ways to make your space work harder to ensure you can squeeze in everything you require and guarantee enough workspace. "You need to have all the essentials, but in compact form," says Rebecca Benichou, founder of Parisian studio Batiik, which specializes in overhauling tiny homes. "For example, a small sink and hob will free up more of your countertop for food preparation." She also recommends seeking

out combined appliances, such as a space-saving oven-and-dishwasher duo. Benichou's preferred design tack is to "hide" the kitchen, integrating it within the existing architecture. "It shouldn't look like a kitchen," she explains. Easier said than done, you might think, but with the right architect, anything's possible. When Angel Rico designed a 20 m² (215 ft²) beachside apartment in Spain for a young family, he hid the kitchen behind a series of moving elements that open out to reveal different functions. Unfolding one part of the design creates a floor-to-ceiling partition, while another wall reveals a deep shelving unit. Behind this is a microwave, hob, and small hotel-style fridge.

When space is really tight, a kitchenette might be sufficient to serve your culinary needs. Flexibility is your friend here, with portable and freestanding options becoming an increasingly attractive option for the spatially challenged. London-based graduate Yu Li recently designed a groundbreaking portable kitchen for millennials: a seven-in-one cooking set comprising a chopping board, an induction →

Architect Angel Rico designed this concealed kitchen for a young family's 20 m² (215 ft²) beachside apartment in Spain. A series of moving elements fold out to reveal different functions, from a floor-to-ceiling partition to a deep shelving unit for crockery and glassware, and various compact appliances.

The kitchen of this Melbourne micro apartment was conceived by owner-architect Nicholas Agius. Based on the concept of a tool box, the oversized cupboard opens up to reveal a sink, oven, hob, and cleverly configured storage. The sunny yellow woodwork adds an unexpected pop of cheerful color.

hob, a pot and pan, a wrap for utensils and cutlery, and a drying rack in one tiny box. While this might just be the smallest solution yet, space-saving kitchens aren't a new invention. In 1963, industrial designer Joe Colombo created his Minikitchen for Boffi that is just as relevant today as it was when conceived. It takes the form of a trolley on castors, and contains a hob, mini refrigerator, storage compartments, cutlery drawers, sockets for electrical appliances, a large chopping board, and a pullout countertop. Larger, but just as clever, is May Kukula's Oikos, a two-wheeled "wagon" that can transform from dining table or desk to kitchen work-bench due to its hidden electrical sockets, induction hob, and integrated storage.

Whether you opt for a built-in or freestanding kitchen, it's worth remembering that adequate ventilation is a key consideration when cooking in an open-plan space. Another important factor is storage, which can be integrated in a wealth of ways, from slender floor-to-ceiling cabinetry to deep drawers. Overhead racks and wall-hung shelving will help to free up floor space, but try to keep excess clutter in check. The less you have on display, the more roomy your kitchen will appear.

Italian industrial designer Joe Colombo created his Minikitchen for Boffi in 1963. The wheeled design contains a hob, mini refrigerator, and storage compartments, as well as cutlery drawers, sockets for electrical appliances, a large chopping board, and a pullout countertop—all in one tiny trolley.

May Kukula's Oikos is a two-wheeled "wagon" that can be easily moved out of the way when not in use. Designed for both homes and offices, Oikos can transform from dining table or desk to kitchen workbench when needed, thanks to its hidden electrical sockets, induction hob, and integrated storage.

213

A Place for Everything

When it comes to small spaces, there's more than meets the eye. Find out how to to make your compact kitchen work harder

Storage is the backbone of any kitchen, particularly a small one. That's why it's vital to find the right solutions to make the most of your space—ones that conceal equipment and appliances, but ensure that they are readily accessible. As urbanization continues to rise, the interiors of small homes are becoming even more exciting, thanks to a wealth of innovative designers and suppliers. Spanish architecture firm *Elii* has spent years honing its craft by developing interior concepts for apartments from its office in Madrid. The team has a particular knack for well-considered refurbishments that use modular dividers, grid-based layouts, and versatile materials to create multi-functional spaces. *Batiik Studio* has a similar eye for function-forward designs tailored for tiny apartments, like those common in its native Paris, using arched cutouts and zigzag lines to create a dynamic sense of motion. Paired with bold color swatches and accent walls, the effect is striking:

quiet and cozy corners are filled with life and light, creating the illusion of a much larger space than that which was available.

Others prefer to conceal their kitchen appliances entirely, and *Sanwa* in Japan offers minimalist designs that do just that. Its hobs, ovens, and range of appliances discreetly blend into a wall of cabinets and shelves while retaining their full functionality. For iconic design brand *Boffi*, blending in was never an option. Here, sleek, stylish kitchen concepts are designed with an eye for visual balance and an emphasis on the Italian craftsmanship that they've been known for since the early 1930s. These kitchens are true to Boffi's Italian roots—ostensibly simple but done to perfection.

A kitchen should be timeless not just in style but in material as well, which is why furniture from *Floyd* is designed to pair ease of assembly with durability. Made from real wood, steel, and linoleum, collections from the American manufacturer are intuitive to build and stylistically cohesive, which means that its tables, counters, and chairs can transition easily from kitchen to living room, or anywhere else. Its furniture is drafted in its in-house research and development lab, and each piece must align to its central core belief that furniture is meant to last for life. Small appliances and fixtures tie together a visual concept, which

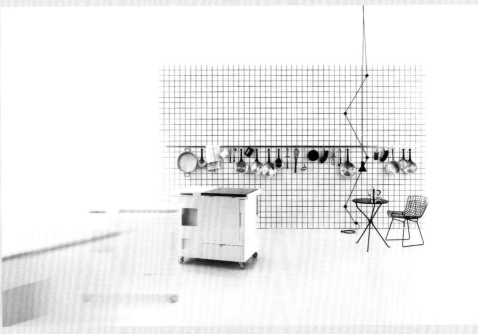

is why companies like Germany's *Blanco* and *Sur La Table* from the States offer a curated selection of finishing touches to complement larger structural supports like the cabinetry and architecture. At the end of the day, a kitchen is to be enjoyed—finding a sturdy and stylish interior concept simply provides peace of mind, and the reassurance that there is a place for everything.

Find the brands, designers, and manufacturers that are carving out their own niche in interior design and architecture for kitchens in our index at the back of the book.

→ Batiik Studio built furniture to fit around and under the windows of this tiny Parisian apartment, creating enough room for a decent-sized kitchen, which includes a double oven, a four-ring hob, and a dishwasher.

How to Cook up a Storm in a Tiny Studio

"The owner of this flat needed a decent-sized kitchen, which was almost impossible in such a small space," says Rebecca Benichou, the architect who designed this tiny Parisian aparment. The solution she came up with was to build furniture to fit around and under the windows, stretching the length of the apart-ment and providing adequate room for storage and appliances.

Far from a kitchenette, the new design squeezes in a double oven, a four-ring hob, and a dishwasher.

In one corner, a floor-to-ceiling okoumé wood cabinet contains a large fridge and a washing machine. Out of the side of this folds a slim panel that serves as both a countertop and a desk. "It's really nice to sit in front of the window and eat or work," Benichou says. And, if a more formal dining arrangement is needed for entertaining, the built-in seat on the other side of the kitchen creates space for a proper dining table for sit-down suppers.

A Minimal Kitchen for a Michelin–Starred Chef

Danish kitchen maker Garde Hvalsøe has spent the past 20 years focusing on what it calls "pure and honest design." The company is headed up by three cabinetmakers and an architect, all of whom are passionate about Nordic design traditions. The kitchen they created for Copenhagen-based chef Nicolai Nørregaard is a testament to this, combining expert craftsmanship with overt simplicity. Having designed the production kitchen for his two-Michelin-starred restaurant, the team was enlisted again to work its magic in Nørregaard's home. The result is a fusion of Danish and Japanese influences, a look that feels well suited to the 1970s architecture of the house. Three rooms were knocked together to create one large, open space for Nørregaard and his family; the kitchen was then fitted with a long bank of cabinetry made from Douglas fir, topped with raw steel work surfaces. A wall of open shelving, filled with ceramics and cookery books, helps to bridge the gap between the cooking and living area.

→ As part of its latest +Venovo range, Poggenpohl created a freestanding kitchen that aims to better suit people's evolving lifestyles. Supported by slender feet, the unit includes all the required functions, such as a hob, oven, extractor fan, refrigerator, and sink.

Innovative Design for Evolving Lifestyles

Founded in Germany in 1892, Poggenpohl is one of the oldest kitchen brands in the world. Its made-to-measure, hand-assembled kitchens fuse high-tech solutions and innovative thinking with time-honored craftsmanship, prioritizing both form and function. "We always consider the space first, rather than the units or cabinets to fill it," says the brand. "This allows our kitchens to function in a more satisfying and ergonomic way." For its latest +Venovo range, Poggenpohl looked to "global megatrends such as urbanisation and mobility." The result is a free-standing design that aims to eliminate the boundary between kitchens and living spaces to suit people's evolving lifestyles. Even better: if you decide to move house, you can take your +Venovo kitchen with you. Supported by slender feet, the unit is designed to "float" in space, minimizing the impact on the wider room. Efficiently configured, it includes all the required functions, such as a hob, oven, extractor fan, refrigerator, and sink.

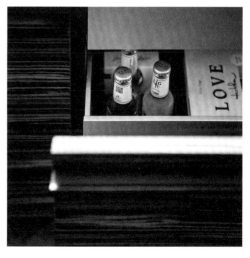

A Sunny Yellow Kitchen Concealed in a Cupboard

Built in 1935 by Australian architect Acheson Best Overend, Cairo Flats is a historic art deco building located in Melbourne's Fitzroy suburb. An early example of micro living, the tiny apartments were initially designed with external cooking, laundry, and communal dining facilities. Fast-forward to present day, and the residences have had to be reconfigured with all the necessary facilities inside, which is why architect Nicholas Agius needed to get creative in order to squeeze a new kitchen into his apartment's compact floor plan.

His solution was to design a "tool box" that opens up to reveal a fully fitted kitchen, complete with a sink, oven, hob, and cleverly configured storage. Two walls conceal the space: one is set on hinges so it can swing open; the other is hung on a rail so it can slide to the side to close off the adjacent bedroom. Smart ideas, like the overhead drying rack, make good use of the pocket-sized kitchen, while the sunny yellow woodwork adds a pop of cheery color.

A Small but Beautifully Organized *Japanese* Kitchen

Precise measurements, bespoke storage, and carefully chosen materials underpin this tiny space in Tokyo

Yuka and Yoichiro Tomioka

→ *Architect Kei Sato chose to make the cooking area of this petite kitchen lower than normal so it could become one with the long dining table that extends off the central island unit.*

When Japanese studio 8 Tenhachi embarked on a new kitchen for the Tokyo home of Yoichiro and Yuka Tomioka, one of the first things architect Kei Sato did was ask for their height measurements. This allowed him to tailor the proportions of the compact kitchen to make it as precise and user-friendly as possible. Sato created the kitchen in collaboration with Yoichiro Tomioka, a product designer for plumbing fixtures. The pair had worked together in the past, so Sato was the perfect choice for the project, which involved creating a small and incredibly practical kitchen with space for living and dining.

Before designing anything new, Tomioka assessed the usability of the existing kitchen and defined the working triangle comprising the fridge, cooker, and sink. Together with Sato, he then came up with a concept that would feel in keeping with the rest of the house. "Our home is very tiny, so I wanted have a simple kitchen that would blend into the original architecture," he explains, referencing the pared-back white-and-wood design. The next step was to configure the space. Sato and Tomioka chose to make the cooking area lower than normal so it could become one with the long dining table that extends off the central island unit. The wet area, on the other hand, was elevated to make washing up a little easier. Lots of storage was built in under the sink unit, which is integrated into a wall of cabinets that hides kitchen appliances and a pantry behind its sliding doors. The same white paint chosen for the cabinetry was also used on the wall, a deliberate decision to help the kitchen slot seamlessly into the existing interior. The color choice also helps to make the space feel larger, as does the amount of concealed

→ *One of the first things Sato did was to take the couple's height measurements. This allowed him to make the space as user-friendly as possible.*

functions, from storage to light switches and a wine glass rack designed to display only the tops of the glasses and bounce light around the sink area.

One of the main challenges the duo faced came as a result of the large ceramic tiles chosen for the countertop, which are durable, heat resistant, and "great for kneading bread," but also very expensive. To tackle this, Tomioko opted to use painted wooden boards (that had been color matched to the ceramic tiles) to clad the sides of the central island and the walls surrounding the sink. "No one ever notices the difference in the materials," he says. "It tricks people into thinking that all the surfaces are made from the expensive gray ceramic tiles."

"Modern Japanese" is how the owners define the overall look and feel of the new kitchen, which has been painstakingly organized to make it suitable for family life. An induction hob minimizes the risk of accidental burns, and safety catches are fitted to all of the cupboards that are within reach of little hands. "The space encourages the kids to get involved in small ways too," Tomioko explains. "For example, our four-year-old boy can now help us to pull out the plates and chopsticks, and put them back. And they love to see what we're doing, particularly if it involves making cookies!" ∎

"*Our home is very tiny, so I wanted to have a simple kitchen that would blend into the original architecture*"

→ *The space has been painstakingly organized to make it suitable for family life. "It encourages the kids to get involved in small ways,"*
Tomioka explains. "For example, our four-year-old boy can now help us to pull out the plates and chopsticks, and put them back."

An Earthy, Rugged Design for a Floating Home

This floating guest lodge, located on a lake in Oxfordshire, was built by British brand Eco Floating Homes. It is made from sustainable materials and features a steel hull and a deep metal ballast for stability on the water. The interior is the work of architectural salvage specialists Retrouvius, who brought in a wealth of salvaged materials and reclaimed wood to give the brand-new building some character. As the home is mainly used by visiting friends and family, the kitchen is equipped only with a portable hob, fridge, and a sink. "It was more about providing the luxury of privacy first thing in the morning and last thing at night, so it's geared towards drinks and snacks rather than main meals," says Maria Speake, architect and co-founder of Retrouvius.

Engineered wooden boards were used for the cabinetry, chosen to weather life on the water, while reclaimed tiles from Bert & May form the backsplash, which blends beautifully with the tones of the timber. The earthy palette extends to every detail, from the aged copper plug sockets to the bronze lights and the brown salt-glazed sink—positioned on top of the waney-edge counter in order to free up more space in the cupboards underneath.

An Ingenious Fold–Out Solution for Micro Living

When a young family asked architect Angel Rico to design the interior of their 20 m² (215 ft²) beachside apartment in Spain, his response was a single, incredibly clever piece of furniture. Rico designed a modular system that can transform the space throughout the day according to its owners' needs, concealing a wealth of functions and storage solutions. "By utilizing vertical space, the design maximizes area and participates in the evolution of micro living," says the architect.

Integrated into the design is a small but perfectly formed kitchen, hidden by various movable elements when not in use. Unfolding part of the wall creates a floor-to-ceiling partition, while another reveals a deep shelving unit for crockery, glassware, and dry goods. Behind this is a kitchenette with a microwave, hob, and small hotel-style fridge. A slim table extends out to seat up to 11 people (at a push), while overhead storage on the balcony holds a series of foldable dining chairs.

Angel Rico

→ *This modular system is designed to help transform this apartment for various different uses. A movable shelving unit opens up to reveal a kitchenette behind, which is fitted with the basic necessities for a small family.*

How a Simple Table Transformed This Home

This spacious kitchen takes up a large portion of architect couple Tomoko Sasaki and Kei Sato's Tokyo apartment, which they renovated to create a more flexible format, stripping back the entire home and removing all partition walls.

At the center of the restructured space is the kitchen, which Sasaki and Sato, who head up Japanese studio 8 Tenhachi, knew would be the heart of their home. Because of this, they decided to create one fluid area for cooking, entertaining, working, and relaxing together as a family. Key to this is a long table made from Japanese cedar: a multi-functional piece of furniture that acts as a dining area, work surface, and desk (for kids and adults alike).

The hybrid piece, which can seat up to 20 people, is an ideal fit for this versatile space. On the far wall, floor-to-ceiling cupboards prevent kitchen equipment from encroaching on the living area, while shelving suspended over the counter allows everyday utensils and crockery to be kept within easy reach.

Sustainable Materials Shine in This Swedish Abode

Located in an aluminum-clad home in Linköping, in southern Sweden, this low-cost kitchen is the work of Björn Förstberg and Mikael Ling of Malmö-based architecture firm Förstberg Ling. Originally conceived for a sustainable-housing competition, the home was designed for Förstberg's mother, Maria. "House for Mother,"

as it is known, is a home that balances "spatiality with intimate rooms" and "formal simplicity with strong materiality," according to the architects, who created a large and inviting kitchen that flows into a living area. A double-height space with exposed beams, the design feels in keeping with its rural location, while the pared-back

material palette is distinctly contemporary—and budget friendly to boot. Pine plywood was used for most of the construction, with some walls and units stained dark for depth and character. A practical stainless-steel counter defines the cooking and prep area, which is fitted with appliances from Ikea, while simple white tiles form the backsplash.

Förstberg Ling

"The house balances *spatiality* with intimate rooms and formal simplicity with strong materiality"

→ White paint was used to define the living area of this open-plan space, the concrete floor of which extends part of the way up the walls to create a low-level bench that wraps around the room.

Atelier Sagitta

Slatted Oak and a Bright Green Scheme

Atelier Sagitta undertook the design of this two-room Parisian apartment for a talented young art director who works in the music industry. His brief for the studio was to bring a touch of originality to the kitchen area, which is always on show, no matter where one is in the small apartment. Naturally, he was also keen to optimize space.

The designers set about reworking the cooking area into the main living space, adding a dining table to the kitchen to free up room in the sitting area. An L-shaped configuration was chosen for the layout, which is comprised of a back wall of storage and appliances, and a line of slatted oak cupboards that "overflow" into the living room—the work of cabinet-maker Michel Mazué. Perhaps most notable is the use of color: a bright emerald green fills the recessed area, which, alongside a change in flooring, turns a functional space into a statement feature.

Emerald green fills the recessed area, turning a functional space into a statement feature

→ *The L-shaped kitchen features bespoke units in pale oak, which contrasts beautifully with the vibrant green walls and cabinetry. The tiny folding dining table and stools are a perfect fit for this compact space.*

Studio Ulanowski

A Sleek and Livable Family Space

When Eryk Ulanowski, architect and founder of Studio Ulanowski, was asked to design a London home for a Hong Kong-based jewelry designer and her family, his main task was to tackle the challenging interior layout, which he describes as "unapproachable and rigid." In its place, he introduced a playful new scheme with unexpected layers of depth.

"In the main living space, the key was to break down the boundaries of living, dining, and cooking, which were compartmentalizing the room," explains Ulanowski. This was done with a number of interventions. The bespoke oak kitchen, made from fluted timber and slabs of gray terrazzo, wraps around the walls, and its lower half is painted pale blue and includes a long run of cabinets that extends into the living area. Here, the dining table can be turned around and extended to seat up to 12 people or become a roomy homework station for the owner's children. Finished in the same oak, the table fits snugly over the living room cabinets so that the two appear to merge into one.

"In the main living space, the key was to *break down* the boundaries of living, dining, and cooking"

→ *This bespoke oak kitchen by Studio Ulanowski is made from fluted timber and slabs of gray terrazzo. A long run of cabinets extends into the living area, and the dining table fits snugly above them so that the two appear to merge into one.*

→ The less-is-more kitchen of this modern chalet is unpretentious and understated, in keeping with the wilderness refuge La Shed was trying to create. Pale wood floors and soft white cabinetry combine, while the large farmhouse table is a nod to country style.

Modern Meets Rustic in This Mountain Home

Bright, open, and comfortable, this new-build home in Quebec's Eastern Townships was designed by Canadian firm La Shed. "A reinterpretation of the traditional Alpine chalet" is how the studio thinks of the house, which fuses artisan techniques with contemporary architectural design. In the kitchen, breathtaking mountain views are hard to ignore, so the interior is deliberately understated, in keeping with the "unpretentious and peaceful wilderness refuge" that La Shed designed for a family of three. A palette of pale wood and soft white keeps the decor simple, as does sleek, handle-free cabinetry. The wall of floor-to-ceiling storage keeps appliances and utensils out of sight, contributing to the less-is-more aesthetic. Past the dining area, large glass doors slide back, opening the space up to the outside, where a wide deck overlooks the pool and the mountains beyond. Subtly traditional touches, such as the long farmhouse table, are a nod to country style, while knotted pine floors add an air of rusticity.

Kitchen *Living*

Kitchen Interiors for Contemporary Homes

This book was conceived, edited, and designed by gestalten.

Edited by *Robert Klanten* and *Andrea Servert*
Contributing editor: *Tessa Pearson*

Preface by *Mina Holland*
Texts written by *Tessa Pearson*

Editorial management by *Sam Stevenson*

Design, layout and cover by *Mona Osterkamp*

Typefaces: Ogg by *Sharp Type*, Nimbus Roman by *URW Studio*, and Aktiv Grotesk by *Dalton Maag*

Cover photography by *Dion Robeson*

Printed by *Printer Trento S.r.l.*, Trento, Italy. Made in Europe

Published by Gestalten, Berlin 2019
ISBN 978-3-89955-965-1

© Die Gestalten Verlag GmbH & Co. KG, Berlin 2019

FSC
www.fsc.org
MIX
Paper from responsible sources
FSC® C015829